THEORY AND REALITY IN WORLD POLITICS

THEORY AND REALITY IN WORLD POLITICS

Carey B. Joynt
and
Percy E. Corbett

University of Pittsburgh Press

First published in Great Britain 1978 by
THE MACMILLAN PRESS LTD

Published in the U.S.A. 1978 by the
UNIVERSITY OF PITTSBURGH PRESS
Pittsburgh, Pa. 15260

Printed in Hong Kong by

Library of Congress Cataloging in Publication Data

Joynt, C. B.
   Theory and reality in world politics.

   Includes bibliographical references and index.
      1.   International relations.   I.   Corbett, Percy Ellwood, 1892–   joint author.   II.   Title.
JX1395.J69   327   77–14693
ISBN 0–8229–1132–9

For Anne, David and Margaret

Contents

Contents

Preface

The authors wish to thank the following for their critical comments: Dr Nicholas Rescher, University Professor of Philosophy, University of Pittsburgh, who read chapters 2 and 9; R. M. Hare, White's Professor of Moral Philosophy, University of Oxford, who read chapter 2; Professor F. H. Hinsley, St John's College, University of Cambridge, who commented on chapters 5—Conclusion; and Dr Alvin J. Rubinstein, Professor of Political Science, University of Pennsylvania, who read portions of the manuscript.

Gratitude is expressed to the publishers Sweet and Maxwell Ltd for permission to reprint portions of two articles which appeared in the *Year Book of World Affairs 1964* and *1978*.

We wish to thank Mrs Doris Wilkinson for her skill in producing the typescript and for her constant good cheer.

I
Introduction

This book is written for an undergraduate audience. It is intended to acquaint the beginning student with the broad range of theory that has been developed and the positive contributions which some theories have made or can make to our understanding of a complex field.

Our choices of materials to be included were dictated by several key considerations. We have chosen to discuss ethical problems and the role of historical studies because these two approaches suffer from undue neglect in most treatments of the subject and because we believe that serious reasons of substance demand their inclusion. The chapter on "Ethics and International Relations" argues that a study of ethical issues is important because many, if not all, political decisions contain hidden ethical choices which need to be analyzed if the choices themselves are to be understood and because many crucial problems, including the origins of war, have a major ethical component.

A plea is made for the uses of history not because history is an easy or infallible guide to an understanding of the present—it is not—but because events take place within a certain framework of time and in a particular pattern. In short, there is a quality of uniqueness in events which occur in history and they therefore require some account of that quality to supplement our understanding. History also provides us with the major source of hypotheses about why and how things occurred in the way they did as well as the data which can be used to falsify or lend credence to our account of events. Finally, history is important because men—including key decision-makers—use its presumed "lessons" as a guide in the conduct of state policy. The impact of Munich and the appeasement period is the best known example of this tendency.

We have made a special effort to avoid the use of jargon and pompous verbiage in the profound conviction that these malodorous practices are largely responsible for the sense of frustration and despair which assails most beginners in the field as well as for a great deal of muddle and obscurity of thought among the theorists themselves. If we have transgressed in any way against these admonitions we beg the reader's forgiveness. We can only plead that even the most determined advocate of lucidity can be worn down by constant immersion in a sea of abstract and enigmatic speculation. But we have done our best to lead the student safely through some tangled thickets. Whether we have done so successfully will be a matter for each reader to decide for himself.

In one other particular the book is unique. It contains a short chapter on the international impact of American theory, the content of which required the careful study of literature in the major European languages, including Russian. With this exception, all the sources surveyed were selected in order to present the student with some introduction to major movements of thought about the subject and to concentrate upon those works which would be available in almost any good college or university library. For this latter reason alone, not from any conviction that good theoretical work began only in the past decade or so, we have tended to emphasize works written in the fairly recent past.

At this point, a word should be said which justifies in general terms the attempt to provide theories about international relations. Why bother about theory at all? The short answer is that even the merest chronology contains an implicit theoretical scheme since certain facts are selected to the exclusion of others. Whenever we attempt to understand and explain events we use a theory. Some kind of theory is therefore a necessity and the only issue is whether it should be carefully delineated or left implicit.

One final thing should be said about the connection between theory and reality in international relations. It is that we can never have a complete theory of the subject, not merely because factors are often present without our knowledge, but because there are always present in politics elements of contingency, irrationality and fortuitous behavior. Every theory is of necessity limited to the study of the rational and recurrent elements in political action. These elements set limits to what theory can do for our understanding. Within these limits it is difficult but not impossible to develop sound and, hopefully, useful theories. Better theories and therefore a better understanding of reality is the chief, perhaps the only, way to a more orderly and just international society since there can be no real control of a situation without a reasonably accurate understanding of it.

2
Ethics and International Relations

It may be thought that to talk of the role of ethics in international affairs is to deal in the irrelevant and the absurd. For after all is it not to be taken as an axiom that the policies of states are guided solely by national self-interest? And yet one wonders if so easy a generalization is wholly true since the subject has been a source of lively debate since the time of Thucydides and shows no signs of disappearing in our own day. The existence of an interest in moral questions and the use of moral terms by statesmen raises the suspicion that the subject is worth at least passing consideration in any study of international relations. What then are the grounds for the belief that ethics may have a role to play in the relations between states?

There are several basic reasons which can be advanced to explain the persistence of moral concerns in the field, some practical and some theoretical in nature. The average citizen takes it for granted that the conduct of governments in their external relations is a proper subject for moral judgments.[1] He persists in condemning governments for acts which he considers wrong or unjust and he commends them for acts he describes as good and upright. Statesmen constantly appeal to moral motives in an effort to secure approval for policies or decisions. Such tactics are a direct admission that people are moved by moral ideals and, therefore, that any simple division between morals and power is based on false premises.

It is no use arguing therefore that, since very different moral positions may be held by governments, moral considerations should be rejected as an influence on foreign policy on the ground that these only irritate foreigners and hinder the peaceful resolution of disputes.[2] Such advice flies in the face of the fact that peoples and nations are moved in fact by moral forces. As long as this is the case statesmen will continue to appeal to moral ideas and just so long will morals play a role in the policies of states. This fact about the world then is a major key to understanding the present and future part played by statesmen as diverse as Roosevelt and Hitler, if not by all analysts of foreign policy. This is why superior moral positions are so much prized in diplomacy that even the most brutal governments make strenuous efforts to fake them.[3] The obligations of democratic governments, of course, go much farther than mere pretense since in democratic political theory the state exists to serve the needs and aspirations of individual citizens, including their moral ideals. In democratic states leaders are induced by opinion to keep policy moving toward moral objectives within the limits of prevailing moral opinions and the life and security of the society. The question then becomes one of estimating the range and degree of impact made by ethical principles and in particular how they affect national policies. A short answer is that there are undoubtedly highs and lows in the attitudes and policies of most countries. The idealism of Woodrow Wilson was followed by the withdrawn mood of the period between the wars but few will deny that the Japanese peace treaty and the Marshall Plan contained a good measure of generosity or that we are now witnessing an erosion in the United States of the public sense of responsibility for improving the lot of peoples in the underdeveloped world. An ebb and flow in moral commitments undoubtedly occurs, affected by the scale of the sacrifices demanded, the perceived results, and the degree of empathy produced by knowledge of actual conditions. In short, moral perceptions are not constant but fluctuate over time.

The second major point at which ethics enters the realm of practical affairs is through the character of those who make policy. Only the most stubborn believer in the dogma of power politics could fail to see significant moral differences in the policies followed by Hitler or Stalin as contrasted with the actions of Woodrow Wilson or Franklin Roosevelt. This is not to deny that even high-minded men may not display qualities of ruthlessness or deception when matters of security are involved—the recent revelations concerning CIA involvement in political assassinations is a shocking example—but only that there are significant differences of degree and emphasis which point to an important role for morals in the life of nations. The part which character plays in political life will be a function of the interplay between the scope allowed for moral action by particular circumstances on the one hand, and the vision and moral sensitivity of the statesman on the other.

The staggering changes that have taken place in the environment of world politics now pose a special challenge to the moral sense of men. The most dramatic examples are the development of nuclear weapons and the missile race on which the great powers are now engaged. Together with the problems of an exploding world population and serious threats to the environment from pollution, these changes have begun to erode the traditional foundations of the nation-state system. For the first time in history clearly demonstrable common interests have emerged which are shared by all humanity. These interests are not merely peripheral to the central concerns of man, but go to the root question of his survival. The problems posed by these developments cannot be resolved by individual state action. They require cooperative policies leading to the creation of a new world order based on justice and peaceful relations. Thus the great challenges of the day are what they have always been—challenges to the moral sense of men. The major difference between the present and the past is that now the greatest ethical question of all has been raised in the most dramatic and demanding manner possible. It is the question "How ought men to live?" and the survival of mankind depends upon the responses made to it.[4]

The second area which must be examined in order to discover the role of ethics lies in the nature of human decisions and the function of moral principles in the sphere of human judgment. This is a subject of great complexity and generations of moral philosophers have explored the subtleties involved in elaborate, sophisticated ways. The result is a thicket so dense that the great American philosopher Charles Peirce once remarked that "nothing makes a man so much of a scoundrel as a prolonged study of ethics."[5] Faced with this situation the nonspecialist can best serve the cause of his readers if he makes his own assumptions and ethical stance as clear as possible, expressed in terms which can be generally understood but which are nevertheless adequate to the purposes at hand.

Our basic position is that ethical principles represent the accumulated wisdom and insight of man with respect to the realization of his true interests. This is not to say that a few simple moral principles exist which can be applied with assurance as guides to action in complex situations. In fact, the contrary is the case. It is "rarely possible to formulate any theoretical principles from which moral rules can be derived such that these rules ought to be observed by everyone,"[6] let alone statesmen. This is so because moral judgments relate to particular situations of extraordinary complexity which demand the application of judgments of diverse types. Simply because the combination of circumstances varies so widely no general rule can be derived which shows the ethical necessity of applying a particular principle. For example, elements in the situation may demand that a particular moral principle be broken. This means that each situation in which a statesman finds himself must be examined separately and with discrimination before moral judgments can be made. Abstract rules are of little use. Rather, moral action consists not in the application of absolute principles in a vacuum but the weighing of conflicting principles in choices which involve problems of power in an effort to act on behalf of preponderant values. No programmatic morality exists. When morality is predetermined or encapsulated in simple maxims, action becomes divided into ineffectual moralism and vulgar expediency.[7] In short, circumstances alter cases, and moral standards should be applied relative to their context. In our case, this means that we can appraise ethical actions in a meaningful way only if we accept the logic of politics as to ends and means.[8]

No one really believes that his choices are illusory or meaningless. At any rate, most people act as if their choices were real choices hammered out on the anvil of decision at great cost to themselves. Such choices are not mere whims, they are made for reasons, and they involve the purposes and objectives of the person making the decision. Once a place for choice is assured in any activity a decision-maker is confronted with two questions: What end or ends should he pursue and what means must he adopt to achieve the ends desired?

The question of what ends are to be pursued is a specifically ethical question. Thus when a choice is made to follow policies aimed at security or peace or plenty an ethical choice has been made. But the question of means is in most cases also an ethical one. Thus, when a statesman declares that, in certain circumstances, force will be used to support his policies, a fundamentally ethical decision has been taken. For in such an instance, a decision-maker is in effect saying that the good to be derived from the pursuit of his objectives outweighs the evils resulting from the use of force. Thus statesmen are willy-nilly ethical agents.

The question of means—that is the methods chosen to achieve purposes and objectives—is basically scientific in character but even in this instance if the choice of means involves injury or evil to other persons the achievement of an objective will involve an ethical decision as well.[9]

At this stage in the analysis a critical point is reached. For it would be quite possible to agree with the above contentions and still argue that ethical decisions are made by and large with the pursuit of power as the ultimate goal of nations. In particular, we confront the claim of the Realpolitik school of thought that the protection and extension of the territorial integrity and political independence of the state are the supreme ends of foreign policy. If these assertions are correct, we would be left at best with a world arena in which purely national ethics clash, each claiming and aspiring to a universal validity.[10]

This is a grossly oversimplified view of the facts as they actually exist and, indeed, a view with dangerous consequences when one realizes that opinions of this sort have influenced a whole generation of American students of the subject. We must therefore weigh this general position with care since a great deal is at stake.

First, while this opinion is set forth with dogmatic certainty and assurance, it reflects a highly questionable interpretation of the past by positing a kind of golden age from the Treaty of Westphalia to the Napoleonic Wars and from the end of that struggle to World War I when nations were supposed, by "a framework of shared beliefs and common values" to have imposed "effective limitations upon the ends and means of their struggle for power."[11] This curious opinion can only be maintained by serious distortions of the historical record. Indeed, the exact opposite of these assertions comes much nearer the truth. During the period in question, reason of state ruled as the supreme principle of foreign policy. Ruthlessness, greed and the hatred spawned by war and violence eroded respect for treaties and for law. Cynicism, deception and fraud dominated diplomacy for long stretches of time, particularly during the *ancien régime* and the era of Napoleon. Limits to the struggle for power did evolve but these were largely a consequence of primitive technology and the lack of adequate communications which together set practical boundaries to the effective waging of war. Despite the primitive nature of the weapons available to them, the princes of the *ancien régime* managed to devastate periodically quite large areas and to sacrifice the lives of large numbers of their hapless subjects.[12]

Nor is one's confidence in Morgenthau's skill in historical interpretation restored by the assertion that the present era of nationalistic ethics claiming universal validity was supposedly "ushered in by Woodrow Wilson's War to make the world safe for democracy" and that conflicts of opposing ethical systems are responsible for tearing the world apart, in contrast to the period when the only issues were territorial expansion and dynastic competition.[13]

One would never think, reading this, that World War I began over issues involving territorial expansion and dynastic competition and that these were quite enough to involve states in horrendous conflict. In short, the war began not as Woodrow Wilson's war but as an old-fashioned conflict arising out of a traditional struggle for power in Europe and was the logical culmination of the system which Morgenthau commends to us. It is equally open to us to interpret the effects of two world wars not as the result of struggles made savage by an attempt to impose a set of beliefs, but as a perfectly logical consequence to the growth of technology, the immense resources available to nations and the strength of modern governmental structures which, when harnessed to a war effort, produced conflicts threatening the survival of entire peoples.

These differences of view are not mere debating points since Morgenthau's interpretation, by exaggerating the differences between past and present, leads to a debilitating form of pessimism which pictures "the nationalistic masses" meeting in the international arena "carrying their idols before them" convinced that they "fulfill a sacred mission ordained by Providence" and by implication going on to final catastrophe. This is the kind of extravagant rhetoric which misleads by destroying perspective and by shifting attention away from the central issues of our time, namely that modern science and technology have developed to the point where they are capable of bringing about the destruction of man, and that these powers are held by separate and sovereign governments.

Morgenthau's analysis of the role of ethics is, therefore, not only an exaggeration at the level of *description* but it also leads to errors of interpretation at the level of *prescription*. The objectives of states are various and complex—security, prestige, prosperity, liberty—and they are always in conflict at some level, particularly at the point where scarce resources are allocated in order to achieve them. The proportions and amount which are devoted to each will vary with the scale of priorities held by decision-makers, and this will be a function of ethical values combined with the estimates made of the nature and extent of international dangers and opportunities.

If it is held that the preservation of the state is the supreme end of government, conclusions are reached on priorities and resources which fit uneasily into democratic political doctrines.[14] For one ought to be quite clear that, despite attempts to qualify the issues, such a position[15] has a decidedly authoritarian bent. The reason is that it stems directly from a tradition wholly alien to the American and British tradition of government.[16] The tradition holds that the prime object of policy is the welfare of individuals organized as a national society. To the extent that it ministers to that welfare, territorial integrity is an instrumental objective to which policy is directed. This means, in effect, that priority is given to people's lives as opposed to their interest in territory and this has led governments to prefer surrender of territory to annihilation. When a recent writer[17] argues that "in formulating policies, the ultimate guide must be their implication for the needs and interests, the welfare and dignity, of individual human beings, rather than for the alleged sanctity of symbols and institutions—important and real though these be," he is being true to the democratic tradition.

The contrary view always runs the danger that power, instead of being conceived of as a means to the attainment of other objectives, becomes the supreme end of politics. Carried to its logical conclusion the result is the leviathan state in which all important human values are gradually swallowed up in the pursuit of power. This is not to say that democratic peoples have been entirely free from failure in the attempt to check the process which begins when ultimate value is attached to the state. But by and large they continue to try to confine within narrow channels the needs and demands of power. A recent example has been the Congressional investigation into the activities of the CIA and the FBI. These activities involved actions which were not only repugnant to ordinary citizens but which were a clear violation of international law and the Constitution of the United States. Knowledge of these abuses of power has resulted in efforts, however belated, to denounce and, hopefully, to eliminate or restrict them. There is an important difference between arguing that the state is the supreme moral good and accepting the full consequences of such a belief on the one hand, and, on the other, while admitting that statesmen operate within a set of severe constraints, insisting on the primacy of individual persons as the focus of policy.

This last point leads naturally on to the question of the nature of moral obligations whether assumed by individuals or governments. All moral obligations have three major features: they are personal; they are voluntary; and they involve in some fashion the welfare or happiness of their object. Only persons can be obligated and this means in essence those capable of giving reasons for acting. Such obligations can be assumed only by consent and cannot be imposed by constraint. Thus an obligation is a personal commitment voluntarily assumed. This is the reason why international treaties signed under duress are not morally binding, even though they may be legally binding under the rules of international law.

Those who dismiss the notion of moral obligations in international relations can be answered by the simple fact that men, including men who constitute governments, do constantly assume the existence of moral obligations and undertake them; and it is clear that one of the reasons for such behavior is the awareness that their actions affect the welfare of their own peoples and that the welfare of the latter is frequently bound up in the welfare of men in other states.

Any realistic discussion of ethics and politics therefore cannot deal with men as if they were individuals in isolation. Men, in fact, live as members of a community, whether the family, the city, the nation or the world community, and in each instance they enter into a complex pattern of mutual relations in a host of matters involving their common welfare. Such patterns involve commitments and these are the foundations for a structure of moral obligation. It is through these patterns of mutual obligation that we derive the important concept that interest forms a part of the binding force of obligation. Duty and interest, therefore, while logically separate, march hand in hand over wide areas of human life. Human experience shows that, in a very large number of cases, it is one's interest to behave morally when one's interests are properly understood. The realist dogma of the inevitable selfishness of national affairs stems from a misguided conception. It is based upon a vew of relationships which holds that one nation's gain is inevitably another's loss and that reciprocity, cooperation and mutual assistance are self-defeating. In actual fact, however, national actions cannot afford to be indifferent to the welfare of others because such indifference to *others'* welfare could be the worst possible way of serving *ours* in a very wide variety of circumstances. Modern technology and communications ensure that states today have a wide area of fundamental interests in common, in trade, science and culture. Perhaps more important, all nations have one supreme common interest—the prevention of a world war fought with atomic-hydrogen weapons which would destroy them all alike. Thus for the first time in history peace and security are becoming co-extensive terms and depend for their actualization upon mutually agreed arrangements. In short, the imperatives of modern science are compelling men to recognize that no simple division exists between interests and morality because everyone has an interest in morality.

It does not, of course, follow that this logic will be followed in the policies of states. Statesmen may decide for reasons of short-term gain to behave selfishly and to base decisions on calculations of immediate expediency. To the extent that they do so they bear witness to the tragic aspects of international life, and, if such conduct is persisted in, they may cause the destruction of civilized life as we know it. Modern military technology, by the manner in which it has combined in inextricable fashion interests and morals, has ensured that immoral actions will be self-defeating in the larger questions of strategy. Human survival as well as progress in human welfare at every level depends upon the recognition that stable communities and world order are built on trust, not mistrust and suspicion, upon the fulfillment of obligations, not callous disregard for the rights of others.

It is often argued that a sharp distinction should be drawn between the ethics of individuals and the ethics of states and that they are, in fact, governed by quite different principles. This view is of ancient lineage and reappears with depressing regularity in modern writings on the subject.[18] A more sensible and defensible view is that the principles are the same but that their application may be different because the circumstances in which they are applied may differ and that hence they may require modification.

For example, the obligations of individuals and states are both limited by the ability to perform the duty concerned. A country unable to feed its own population has no obligation to feed the starving in other lands, and in this respect its duties resemble the obligations of poverty-stricken individuals.

Both individuals and states face conflicting obligations. For example, both may face the need to lie in order to avoid greater evils which would result from a strict reliance on the obligation to tell the truth. Thus, in the spring and summer of 1949 Sir Stafford Cripps denied on several occasions that the pound sterling was to be devalued, even though he knew perfectly well that such a course of action was under consideration. This was ethically defensible since a truthful answer would have let loose a wave of currency speculation which would have caused severe damage to the British economy. This is an application of the principle of choosing lesser evils and is justifiable if such action can be reasonably calculated to avoid more serious calamities. This point illustrates a major factor common to most ethical situations, namely, that we cannot simply apply abstract principles to situations, because in so doing we ignore circumstances which may make it a duty to break the rule.[19] If we extend this analysis to other ethical situations we discover that we must include a host of factors peculiar to each particular situation before arriving at a moral judgment. In the process we discover that no principle or rule has universal validity and that none can be safely applied in abstraction from the concrete circumstances of each case.

It is a sound ethical maxim for private citizens as well as statesmen to beware equating evil that we may speculate *may* occur in the future with pain that we *know* for certain would occur now. If, for example, one had asked in the 1949–52 period whether the United States could justifiably have attacked the Soviet Union with atomic bombs before the latter had acquired a stock of nuclear weapons, in order to avoid possible future extinction, the answer is clear. The United States government knew at the time with certainty that enormous destruction and countless deaths of innocent people would result. It could not possibly be known, however, whether the United States would ever be attacked by the Soviet Union. Unforeseeable circumstances might arise to change Soviet behavior, the technological possibilities might be completely revolutionized by new scientific advances or the Soviets might rest content with mutual deterrence as has indeed proved to be the case. It was a moral obligation, therefore, not to attack because a nuclear assault upon the United States was only a possible future danger whereas the opposite decision was certain to bring suffering and death to millions.

There is, of course, a difference between individual and state responsibilities at one crucial point, although even here the difference is one of degree only. The state, unlike the individual in most orderly societies, is forced to act in a world in which law is not enforced except by the parties themselves. Therefore, in an anarchic international world states can establish reasonable claims to resist aggression and maintain their claims, always provided that honest efforts have been made to exhaust the peaceful procedures open to them. Thus, in effect, a kind of special exemption is created in the case of state action, although this does not mean that states are freed from all restraints and can or should disregard moral considerations.

There are several reasons why this is so, the main one being that to conceive of state behavior in international relations as freed from restraints is to posit a false autonomy of action. In fact, states must consider the effects of reciprocal action by others and this involves a careful weighing of how their decisions affect the future international scene. Violation of commitments, disregard for the rights of other states and unrestrained use of force lead to instability in the environment and ultimately react upon the interests of the violator. This view of the duties of states is often described as "enlightened self-interest" which is simply another way of introducing moral values into political decisions. It is, of course, another example of the inextricable mingling of morals and prudence which produces the web of community and which links the interests of individual states and the wider international order. This is not to say that such moral perceptions always prevail. In fact, they do not. The degree to which they do is partly a function of the moral sensitivity of statesmen and the degree of risks and costs which the decision entails. In general, the greater the risk and cost of the moral demand (particularly in security matters) the more likely it will be that statesmen will choose to ignore the imperatives of ethics. At this point the argument becomes a question of fact, about what the risks and costs really are, what the real room for choice is in particular situations and what the likely consequences of action with varying degrees of moral content is likely to be. It is difficult to see what other general conclusions can be derived from a study of such situations except that dogmatic views, whether based on idealism or cynical power politics, are not justified.

We have yet to consider the argument that statesmen, because they are trustees for the welfare of their own people, are compelled to act in accordance with principles which are different from those which guide the ordinary citizen. This view of the matter is much too simple since it is quite clear that individuals too act as trustees for the welfare of those for whom they bear a special responsibility. Fathers who undertake the support and education of a family are not likely to feel free to devote all their resources to charity and in this respect their moral dilemma resembles the kind of choices which confront statesmen. Both must balance conflicting claims and try to do what is right. Both, in short, are occupying a role which makes special moral demands upon the occupant. The chief difference between the two is that the father's role is personal and face-to-face whereas the role of the statesman is more structured and involves a diminution in the face-to-face content of relationships.[20] This means that in practice the temptation grows to treat individuals as means and not ends, the consequences of one's action widen continually as one ascends the hierarchy of power and the pressures to give moral considerations less play also increase progressively. In short, the tasks of authority and the demands of complex organizations tend to become based more and more on mere prudence and the moral content of behavior tends to be compressed by the pressures of time and *raison d'état*. The result all too often is an individual torn between his conscience and the official demands of his office. In such situations the end result can be tragic both for the person and the state he serves if the decision-maker forgets that he is first of all a human being who has a unique obligation to his own moral convictions. When the opposition between private and public duties becomes extreme, when actions mandatory from the one standpoint are ruled out by the other, the statesman must resign if he is to be true to himself. John Bright did so after the British bombardment of Alexandria in 1882 and he was right to do so. We have recently had examples of men who stayed in high office despite the fact that they disagreed with the policies of President Johnson in Vietnam. Both they and the nation were thereby deprived of the opportunity to air legitimate moral and political differences and the result was that policies which had aroused opposition within the government itself were continued past the point where the judgment of the nation should have been sought as to their wisdom. It can be argued, therefore, that the maintenance of the primacy of the personal obligation of statesmen is a necessary condition for the effective workings of democracy. Once more we find that duty and interest march hand in hand and the attempt to divorce the two often leads to serious losses both for the group at large and the individual.

Among the ethical issues posed by the conduct of state relations, none is fraught with such grave consequences as that of nuclear deterrence. It should be said clearly and unequivocally at the outset that no clear guidelines for the just disposition or use of nuclear force exist, nor, by the very nature of the case, is such a code likely to evolve.[21] The truth is that nuclear weapons have confronted us with choices which have destroyed the classical distinctions concerning the just employment of force, and, at the same time, eroded the traditional claim of the state to moral authority over its citizens.[22] This claim rests upon the ability of the state to assure the general safety of its citizens and the integrity of the society of which they form a part. This assurance no longer exists. No reasonable guarantee can be given by any government that the nuclear deterrent will not fail, or that, if it does, the results will be limited in their effects. This is so for many reasons: the inability to specify what constitutes unacceptable damage, the ever-present danger of miscalculation stemming from the interactions of competitive deterrent forces and the lack of means to control the effects of new military technology. In other words, no rationally clear and demonstrable propositions can be advanced to show either that nuclear deterrence is a stable phenomenon or that, if it broke down, the results would not be catastrophic for the populations concerned. These facts are unique in the annals of mankind and it is not surprising therefore that they present ethical and political dilemmas of unprecedented magnitude.

Exactly the same process of erosion can be seen at work if we examine the traditional criteria on the just employment of force. Those criteria held that the prospective destruction involved must be proportionate to the end of upholding justice, that there be a strong expectation that the use of force would succeed in the latter purpose and that noncombatants be immune from attack. All of these criteria are called into question by the deployment of nuclear force which depends for its efficacy upon the threatened destruction of the lives of millions of innocent citizens.

What ends indeed are so precious that they justify the destruction of whole societies? To say that one should choose the death of millions rather than accept survival at the price of subjection to tyranny is neither a powerful nor an appealing argument. For against the certainty of the massive infliction of suffering and death one would have to weigh the possibility, however far-distant and faint, of an escape from bondage into freedom. Certainly there is little reason to believe that the use of hydrogen weapons would lead to a just and durable peace. The far more likely result would be global devastation on such a scale that no rational estimate

could be made of its social and political consequences, to say
nothing of the biological damage resulting from radioactivity. "No
justification for having started a total nuclear war will be accepted
after the event" and no such justification for waging such a war
is acceptable now.[23]

But what are we to make of the argument that the *threat* of
the use of nuclear weapons is a very different thing from their
actual use and that such a policy has a certain measure of justification? In this connection it could be pointed out that the great
powers have not in fact used nuclear weapons in the conflicts
which have occurred since 1945 and it seems entirely reasonable
to suppose that the main factor responsible for the avoidance of
general war has been the awareness of possible escalation due to
the existence of hydrogen weapons. Moreover, it does seem to
be a reasonable conjecture that unilateral surrender of the nuclear
deterrent might well result in nuclear blackmail or perhaps even
the use of such weapons against one's own undefended cities. The
moral issue then becomes whether the risks of a breakdown in
deterrence outweight the clear-cut advantages of the present relatively
invulnerable second-strike systems. In short, there may be a moral
justification in accepting the danger of a collapse in nuclear deterrence
in the interests of preventing the use of such weapons against
one's own society.

This argument has a measure of validity but only if it is clearly
recognized as a choice of lesser evils and as a risk which ought
to be tolerated only in the short run. In the long run there can
be reasonable safety only in a world of states disarmed to police
levels, with the use of force controlled by the political institutions
of a world community. This is a moral imperative because no
deterrent system can be stabilized by the automatic processes of
technology. A just peace can only rest in the final analysis on
a political basis. The deterrent has to fail only once to be fatal
and those who are prepared to run the risks of its failure cannot
logically refuse to run risks for peace in the area of arms control
and disarmament since some possibility of a breakdown always
exists. This is another way of saying that the achievement of a
just peace is the highest ethical imperative. A stable nuclear deterrent
structure, important though it is, can only be a proximate solution
to the problem. Similarly, a restriction of strategy to attacks on
purely military targets, while it would be preferable in an ethical
sense to a counter-city deterrence policy, remains only a palliative.

Another more general problem remains to be discussed: the ethical
problems posed by limited war. The arguments advanced to defend
the limited use of force can be put somewhat as follows:[24] Limited
war raised ethical questions which can be answered only on the

basis of a conception of the proper relation of power and policy. Since human shortcomings make force (and its restraint) imperative, the aim should be not to abolish force but to mitigate and control it for social purposes. These purposes are the ends of national policy and it is vital that military objectives be subordinated to national ends through objective calculations concerning the most effective methods of attaining concrete, limited and attainable security objectives. The political ends of military action must be moral ends. No greater force should be employed than is necessary to achieve the desired political objectives. The entire process of balancing ends and means, of coordinating military with non-military means, must be subordinated to the controlling purpose of pursuing national policy objectives according to the most effective strategic plan. Clausewitz' dictum that war is a continuation of political intercourse is the only view in accord with universal moral principles and consistent with the use of force as a means rather than an end.

A number of objections to this view can be raised. In the first place, national ends in such a scheme are not made subject to ethical adjudication and examination. They are accepted as given ultimates, and are, apparently, considered to be intrinsically moral, for the argument clearly maintains that the justification for the use of even limited power must be some sort of moral end or ends. Surely this failure to discuss the justification of national political ends or objectives simply begs the whole question, for if these ends are immoral then the use of force to defend them is immoral also. Indeed, it is difficult not to draw the conclusion that the final consequence of the failure to subject national objectives to evaluative analysis is to end up with a power-politics theory, albeit in disguise.

Secondly, it is true that limited war is a lesser evil than total war and therefore must be preferred to it. Such a moral choice means that states must prepare themselves to fight limited wars. It would be highly immoral to neglect such preparations and to rely solely upon the fear of the nuclear deterrent to preserve peace and a minimum of justice.

Even when the United States possessed overwhelming superiority in nuclear bombs and delivery systems the threat of retaliation did not prevent local wars and attempted changes in the balance of power. Now that both sides have roughly equivalent means of retaliation a diplomacy based on atomic threats has become unproductive and highly dangerous. This is so because it involves in a peculiarly intense fashion the prestige and, therefore, the credibility of the parties. Once engaged in such a process of threats and counter-threats it becomes difficult to give way for fear that concessions might be interpreted as a failure of nerve and that one's future position might be undermined in a new crisis.

The limited use of force is infinitely to be preferred to such a prospect. But limited war is not the safe haven, either practically or morally, that it is sometimes held out to be. For what grounds do we have for assurance that wars can be kept limited indefinitely either in terms of geography, weapons or objectives?

The picture of two great powers competing for influence in the Middle East, Africa and Southeast Asia by means of intervention in civil strife with large-scale arming of combatants and even the use of their own conventional forces does not provide much assurance of international stability, to say the least. It seems just as reasonable to suppose that, having invested large amounts of resources to obtain their objectives, the powers would be led to increase their commitments and eventually to dangerous confrontations. The best that one could hope for under such circumstances would be a series of stalemates at ever higher levels of cost and danger. Certainly, there is every reason to think that a state which had suffered a series of local losses would, at some point, declare "Thus far and no farther." Some particular issue would assume an importance far outweighing the value of the objective considered in isolation and a decision would be made to stand firm at all costs. Neither side would be willing to watch the world balance of power move decisively against it without running terrible risks in order to prevent a defeat. For, while it would be irrational to pose a nuclear threat to an opponent who possessed a decisive local military advantage, there can be no assurance either that such an irrational decision would not be taken or that local superiority would always obtain. For the desperate gambler or the demonic aggressor the fact would remain that limited conflict operates at only one remove from the diplomacy of nuclear threats and the latter could always be resorted to in a crisis.

Again, all suggestions for limited war which have so far been made envision the erection of a set of rules which are communicated to the opponent in advance.[25] These schemes have a number of common features—they all involve rules which give a distinct advantage to the home side and they all fail to give convincing reasons why the rules would be observed in every instance. In practice such rules are worked out in the midst of a crisis and hence misunderstandings and miscalculations are an ever-present possibility.

Limited war, therefore, can only be defended, like the great deterrent, as a temporary expedient. It must never be forgotten that it is only a stop-gap. If the powers continue to drift desperately from one expedient to the next, frantically trying to prevent or achieve local gains in a series of fluid power situations, peace will remain insecure and the hope of averting a calamitous conflict will remain frail and uncertain.

In conclusion, we must face the fact that it is men's values and ultimately their ethical beliefs which are the basic causes of threats to the peace. For it is their desire to keep the protection of these values in their own hands which ultimately leads to the use of force. In the face of the discoveries of science, this claim of the nations to be final judges in their own cause is a potential source of suicide for all men everywhere. The failure of statesmen, particularly the leaders of the great powers, to admit the implications of the revolutionary nature of modern weapons and to face the full sweep of their political implications is the great immorality of our age. The concept of uncontrolled national sovereignty, which means at bottom the claim to make war, is a death sentence. If decent citizens and their leaders continue to fail to face this fact about the world, they will be confronted at some point with ultimate decisions for which there are no ethical answers. If they abdicate their function as moral men and continue on their present course they will face the need to take actions which are a complete denial of all ethical values. This is the specter presented by the possible breakdown of deterrence. Measures to stabilize deterrence and control the arms race or the ability to fight limited conflicts, necessary and important though they may be, are all inherently inadequate to the challenges presented by modern weapons. Only an advance to a world order equipped with a workable set of institutions to deal with the problems of peaceful change can meet the needs of mankind in the age of modern science.

3
Ideas of Justice in the Relations of States[1]

I THE JUST WAR DOCTRINE

How long the idea of justice has flourished in the literature and oratory of inter-state relations may be judged from Cicero's pronouncements in *De republica* III, 23, and *De officiis* I, 34–5. It was just and legal to make war, Cicero declared, only to avenge wrong, to exact anything due, or to repel an attacking enemy. Moreover, there must be no resort to force until a formal declaration had given the offender the chance to make peaceful amends. Here was the core of the traditional law of nations, which, even as late as the nineteenth century, was predominantly concerned with war. St Augustine endorses Cicero's conditions as, two centuries later, does Bishop Isidore of Seville. Incorporation of the doctrine in the *Decretum Gratiani* (ca. 1140) marks its established place in canon law. Its practical significance is another question.

War was the great preoccupation of the sixteenth- and seventeenth-century jurists, who began the flow of literature on a system of law for the governance of sovereigns. To lessen its frequency and mitigate its horrors was their common objective. There were of course plans, some of them emanating from royal courts, that aimed to eliminate war, at least among Christian peoples, by international organization. But these belonged to the realm of romance. The serious and sustained effort of the jurists was to persuade the rulers of kingdoms and republics not to go to war without just cause and to conduct hostilities as humanely as possible in a clash of arms. Reinforcing the plea for moderation on the battlefield was warning that a war justly begun might be made unjust by the manner of its conduct.

The history of war fails to show any profound influence of these exhortations, either as preventives or as mitigants, on the behavior of governments. The jurists themselves, as time went on, invested the just war doctrine with such a mass of casuistic qualifications that even the frail deterrent of adverse judgment faded to vanishing point. The great difficulty for a humanist like Hugo Grotius who, having narrowly escaped martyrdom for his religious and political views, became an active diplomatist and a world-renowned jurist, was the sharp contradiction between the "natural law" that condemned unjust war, and the law of nations resting upon the consent of states as manifested in their practice. So, while his great treatise, *De jure belli ac pacis*, relied heavily on the old distinction between just and unjust war prescribed by natural and canon law, he found it necessary to admit that the concordant practice of governments accepted "all wars declared by sovereign authority on both sides" as "lawful in their external effects." (Book II, C.XVII, Sec. 19.) This opinion was set down in the first half of the seventeenth century. Yet the literature clung to the distinction for at least another hundred and fifty years. In the 1750s we find the great Emmerich de Vattel wrestling with the problem. As a product of what he calls "the natural and necessary law of nations," the distinction between just and unjust war is binding only in conscience. Both sides may believe in the justice of their claims and, since states are sovereign, none is lawfully entitled to judge another. This was high authority for the abandonment of the just war doctrine in the prevailing positivism of the nineteenth century. Until the Covenant of the League of Nations and Charter of the United Nations attempted to revive and enforce the distinction, the literature of international law, from John Jacob Moser (1701–85) on, almost universally took the position that no legal distinction between belligerents could be based upon their reasons for resorting to force.[2]

The attempts made in the League Covenant (Articles 10–17) and in the UN Charter (Articles 1, 2, 33–53) to prevent aggressive war while preserving the right of self-defense resume in a more practical form the ancient effort to limit war to just causes. If the Charter is to be regarded as part of the law of nations, then the nineteenth-century rule according equal legality to belligerents has been abrogated. Collective pressure against delinquents has been provided for and, in Korea and elsewhere, actually practised. But interminable conflicts dividing the great powers, the special exemptions secured to them by their veto, and multiplication of rabid nationalisms, all combine to cripple the structure of sanctions, and war irrespective of justice continues to slaughter the innocent.

II JUSTICE IN THE GENERAL RELATIONS OF STATES

The appeal to justice in the context of war is only the most ancient of the uses to which the concept has been put in international relations. In our day, justice is invoked and injustice charged in every field of interchange—political, legal, economic, social and cultural—and this practice displays a general belief that justice and law are distinct categories. Justice, in other words, is invoked as a standard of conduct not necessarily satisfied, either in the national or in the international sphere, by mere conformity with law. It is not a rule of law but a moral principle to which law more or less approximates.

Already in the nineteenth century governments embarked upon "humanitarian interventions" against the application of what they considered unjust laws by foreign states even when the victims were nationals of those states. At the same time the principal European powers and the United States insisted upon an abstract standard of justice, as opposed to equality with nationals, in the treatment of aliens.

These assertions of justice, usually by strong against weaker states, were no exception to the general truth that, in an arena without any over-all authority either to determine or to enforce rights and duties, each government defined, and to the extent of its powers exacted its "just claims." In matters where governments discerned a vital interest, the actual state of affairs corresponded closely to the harsh adage that "might makes right." This did not exclude a broad range of routine interchange normally conducted day by day in accordance with pre-established rules. Any part of this interchange might, however, be lifted by special circumstances into the category of vital interest and thus escape control.

The situation today, after two world wars and two laborious attempts to establish the principles and construct the machinery of an operative community of mankind, bears all too close a resemblance to that prevailing in the nineteenth and early twentieth centuries. Violence still rages in the relations between states, and its destructiveness in terms of human life and welfare overshadows the positive accomplishments of the agencies established since 1918 with a view to controlling the use of force and securing the reign of justice. The imperatives of the sovereign state still take precedence over those of an inchoate world community.

If there is one general lesson to be learned from the experience, first of the League of Nations and then of the United Nations, it is that the transition from a world of war and arbitrary power to one of peace and justice, if it is to be achieved at all, cannot but be slow and intermittent. We know now how deeply ingrained are tribal and national attachments and how easily the underlying xenophobia of a people can be inflamed and manipulated by politicians for national or personal ends. Only a profound change in the present thought-patterns and objectives of governing elites and in the political attitudes of their constituents can pave the way to an operative community of man. The basic problem is not one of structure, though structure is of course indispensable, but of developing the world-community mind. In the necessary process of education, analysis of the work of international agencies and of the changes which, in spite of recurrent defeats, they have been able to bring about on the international plane, will be invaluable. One obstruction to be kept under constant attack is the ignorant, escapist or "realist" habit of shrugging off these changes as feeble gestures against the invincible realities of power politics.

What then is the positive record of organization for international peace and justice in the last fifty years?

With all the cautious reservations of state sovereignty that were to be expected from the tradition-bound statesmen of the day, the Covenant and machinery of the League of Nations were a long step towards a supranational polity. The members pledged themselves to submit disputes "either to arbitration or judicial settlement or to inquiry by the Council," and "in no case to resort to war until three months after the award by the arbitrators or the judicial decision, or the report by the Council." They agreed to impose sanctions upon Covenant-breakers. They set up the Permanent Court of International Justice, the first tribunal of its kind in history. They undertook "to secure just treatment of the native inhabitants of territories under their control." They established the mandate system for "the well-being and development" of "peoples not yet able to stand by themselves under the strenuous conditions of the modern world," recognizing such assistance as "a sacred trust of civilization." They also pledged themselves to the endeavor "to secure and maintain fair and humane conditions of labor for men, women and children, both in their own countries and in all countries for which their commercial and industrial relations extend. . . ."

The Covenant formed the first part of the Treaty of Versailles. Part XIII of the same treaty was the constitution of the International Labor Organization. Declaring that there can be no peace without "social justice," this text asserted that labor conditions existed that imposed a degree of "injustice, hardship and privation" incompatible with world harmony. Under the driving direction of Albert Thomas, the organization established to combat these evils set vigorously to work on the long and complex task of liberalizing labor conditions the world over.

Policies and events culminating in the war of 1939–45 destroyed the League of Nations. The International Labor Organization, representing as it does not only governments but organized employers and workers, had won a measure of recognition as an indispensable agency of social and industrial development that defied dissolution. It survived to become the first associated agency of the United Nations under a revised constitution of 1946 which dedicated it to a program of broad humanitarian activity based upon the proposition that "all human beings, irrespective of race, creed or sex, have the right to pursue both their material well-being and their spiritual development in conditions of freedom and dignity, of economic security and equal opportunity." How broadly it has interpreted its mission can be judged from its part in such an enterprise as the Andean Indian Program. There, in collaboration with FAO, WHO and UNESCO, it designed and carried into operation the combination of agricultural, educational, health and welfare institutions needed to start a population of seven million Indians, divided among five states and existing in primordial destitution, on the way to modern living.

Typical of the kind of nationalistic opposition that even the most beneficent international organization encounters is the action taken by the President of the American Federation of Labor in 1971 when, exploiting an accusation of communist domination of the ILO, he persuaded Congress to suspend the United States' quota of financial support.

Professor B. V. A. Roling[3] notes an increasing tendency in international organizations to rely on justice rather than law. Certainly the greatest international organization is charter-bound to seek justice, and it is perhaps significant that justice precedes law in the texts where they stand side by side. Thus the preamble to the United Nations Charter recites in its third paragraph the determination of the peoples of the United Nations "to establish conditions under which justice and respect for the obligations arising from treaties and other sources of international law can be maintained." Again, Article 1 prescribes as one of the first purposes of the organization that of bringing about "by peaceful means and in conformity with the principles of justice and international law, adjustment or settlement of international disputes or situations which might lead to a breach of the peace." Finally, it is justice rather than law that is to be maintained under Article 2, para. 3, which prescribes that "All members shall settle their international disputes by peaceful means in such a manner that international peace and security, and justice, are not endangered."

It is not surprising that the United Nations and its agencies should, especially in recent years, find the appeal to justice more productive than the citation of law. Many of the members have emerged from colonial status only in the last twenty-five years, and their governments do not regard themselves as necessarily bound by rules which they had no part in framing. Only ten of them had, by the end of 1974,[4] accepted the compulsory jurisdiction of the International Court of Justice. There is apparently no general confidence among them that a tribunal applying law established by colonial powers and manned disproportionately by nationals of those powers will offer that protection of the weak against the strong which is the substance of equality before the law and a prime function of courts of justice.[5]

It is to justice again, not to existing laws of commercial and financial interchange, that the scores of underdeveloped peoples must appeal for the technical and economic assistance that only the advanced countries can afford.

But what is justice? From Plato and Aristotle to the present day, volumes have been written in the attempt to win acceptance of a universally valid definition.[6] We do not propose to review that long quest.

The slow working out of an operative code of justice, evolving out of the concrete social relationships of men, demonstrates clearly the essential nature of justice: it is a matter of fairness, the attempt to strike a balance among competing claims. At the present time the claims being advanced in the interests of the world community cluster round the notions of "survival of civilization," "equality of opportunity" and "equitable distribution of the necessities of life." It is therefore no accident that the use of force is regarded as the very negation of justice in contrast to rules of reciprocity and mutual respect or that a consensus is beginning to emerge on the development of a minimum standard of well-being for the peoples of the world.

What we shall attempt is to demonstrate the practical meaning of this standard of conduct as it is revealed in the statutes and activities of the international agencies now dedicated to enhancing the welfare and the dignity of the human individual everywhere. Something in the nature of an operative code is now being worked out on a world scale; and this enterprise, persistent in the face of formidable obstacles, is one of the striking new features of international relations today.

It should be emphasized that while the code aims at universality, it cannot prescribe a detailed uniformity of practice. What seems forgotten in many international charges of injustice is the inevitable variation in the substantive meaning of justice as between radically different cultures. This variation is not overlooked in the United Nations Charter. The importance of cultural diversity in the determination of what is just is recognized, for example, in Article 73, para. a, where states administering the territory of non-self-governing peoples are required to "ensure, with due respect for the culture of the peoples concerned, their political, economic, social and educational advancement, their just treatment, and their protection against abuses."

These cultural variations are not, however, to exceed certain limits. This has been recognized in international relations for at least a century and a half, as the succession of anti-slavery treaties, and the more recent conventions prohibiting institutions and practices akin to slavery, testify. It is the business of the relevant international agreements and agencies to define the required limits. The human individual is to be neither universally homogenized nor yet the entire creature of any specific culture.

The thrust of the concept of justice for those who drafted the United Nations Charter can be seen both in the preamble and in the operative text. We have already quoted passages stipulating the pursuit of justice. The following excerpts show something of the direction the pursuit is to take:

(a) The second paragraph of the Preamble is an undertaking "to reaffirm faith in fundamental human rights, in the dignity and worth of the human person, in the equal rights of men and women and nations large and small."
(b) Article 1, paragraph 2 of the text declares the purpose "to develop friendly relations among nations based on respect for the principle of equal rights and self-determination of peoples."

These two passages make it clear that equality ranked first among the meanings of justice in the minds of those responsible for their wording. But, since physical and intellectual equality among human beings, if indeed desirable, is obviously too remote to serve as a practical aim, what is contemplated is equality of opportunity, in so far as this can be secured by education, health and employment services, the prevention of discrimination on grounds of race, sex, religion or political views, and equality of treatment by legal authorities. This latter—equality before the law—is the one clear meaning of equality for peoples, and it must be conceded that the principle is abandoned in the Charter itself where, as in the Security Council veto (Art. 27(3)) and in the matter of amendments (Art. 108), the great powers are given a legally privileged position.

A great deal of United Nations effort has gone into specifying in concrete detail "the fundamental human rights," and some into the attempt to secure their observance. The results, though far short of the hopes entertained in 1945, are by no means negligible. As for the "rights of nations large and small," the rapid progress of decolonization and the vigorous drive channeled through the United Nations for self-determination in general have changed the entire domain of world politics, both in the number and character of its actors and in the nature of its activities.

In 1948, while the Organization still numbered fewer than sixty member-states, the General Assembly adopted the Universal Declaration of Human Rights. Forty-eight members voted for this elaborate statement of the elements of justice for every human being. There was no adverse vote; but the entire Soviet bloc, plus Saudi Arabia and South Africa, abstained.

The Declaration has been broadcast to the world. Its panoply of rights for the individual surpasses anything yet achieved in the most advanced nations. Nevertheless, it is serving its intended purpose. Being a resolution of the General Assembly, it does not pretend to make laws, it merely formulates "a common standard of achievement for all peoples and all nations." A large number of states have adopted it in their constitutions; it provided the inspiration and much of the text for the Rome Convention on Human Rights; and it has served as a constant model for agencies of the UN called upon to assist members in establishing the rules and procedures of today's welfare state.

Why did the Soviet Union and its allies not vote for so popular a proclamation? Since, as they have always insisted, such products of the Assembly do not make law, they could have supported it with impunity. But could they lend their names to a document formulating such rights as that of private property, freedom of opinion, expression and assembly, to say nothing of the liberty at will to leave one's country and return to it? What they relied on most in the amendments that they have moved and lost in committee was the alleged danger of fascism in societies offering such liberties.[7]

Not content with drafting a declaration, the United Nations Commission on Human Rights was already at work in 1947 on drafts that would create international law in this attractive field. The difficulties encountered in this task and the time taken to prepare texts for submission to the General Assembly, and thence to the members for ratification, reveal the differing degrees of caution exhibited by states when they are asked to join in binding commitments and when the proposal is a mere declaration. With the best will in the world, it is one thing to rally round a statement of resounding aims and quite another to undertake to embody it in national legislation. The generous resolution is, moreover, a tempting way to win gratuitous approbation. Assuming for the moment that forty-eight members of the 1948 United Nations genuinely aspired to the ideal polity depicted in the Universal Declaration, and that the document thus constituted an 84 per cent consensus on the features of such a polity, it is still questionable whether anything approaching this percentage of the doubled membership of 1966 seriously contemplated assuming the legal obligations of the Covenants on Legal and Political and on Social Rights approved by the General Assembly in 1966 and referred to the states for ratification or accession. Many of the new members would be glad to go as far as an Assembly vote in order to emphasize the Covenant's incongruous assertion of a right of self-determination for all peoples and their unrestricted sovereignty over their natural resources. But it is significant, to say the least, if not ominous, that by 28 December 1975 only forty-two states had given their binding consent by ratification or accession to instruments formulated with such prolonged labor and approved by a vote of 105 to 0, Economic and Social, with no abstentions, and 106 to 0, Civil and Political, with no abstentions, in the General Assembly.[8] If the test of serious purpose is subsequent practice, then, with all due allowance for unforeseen problems, it would seem that an impressive show rather than a firm plan of action was a common objective among the official representatives voting in the General Assembly for the Covenants of 1966.

The human rights movement is not confined to the UN and its agencies. We have already referred to the Rome Convention of 1950 which set up the European Commission and Court of Human Rights. This is the strongest organization in the field. Eleven states have granted it authority to deal with private petitions and have given the Court jurisdiction to decide upon complaints referred to it by the Commission or by other states parties to the Convention. The latter body has screened out masses of inadequately substantiated appeals; but those that have been admitted have been effectively dealt with.

The European example is being followed in the Organization of American States. As early as 1959 an Inter-American Commission on Human Rights was created and this has been repeatedly used in the examination of abuses reported by individuals and groups in at least eight of the Latin American Republics. At San José, Costa Rica, on 22 November 1969, twelve states signed a draft convention providing for an Inter-American Court of Human Rights.

All these drives to achieve peace and justice regionally and universally add up to much less than a dominant force in today's world. The enthusiasm for a new era following World War II, like that of the early League of Nations days, was soon dampened by resurgent nationalism. It had never been shared by the Soviet Union, which from the beginning has conceded little power to the UN, where it found itself in a built-in minority and was able only by repeated veto to avert action inimical to its ideology and policy.

Yet, while far from dominant, the pressure for international protection of the individual and for a more equitable distribution of the necessities and amenities of human life continues. The rapid addition of hungry countries to the membership of the UN has kept their demands to the fore in that organization and in its proliferating social, economic and cultural agencies. At the same time the international and internal dissensions of the developing countries, coupled with explosive population growth, add enormously to the difficulties of progress. Nor is it clear that the governing elites of those peoples that would gain most from an effectively organized world community are any more disposed than those of the advanced nations to subordinate their particular interests to any collective purpose.

In the last ten years the dominance of subjectively defined national interests has become especially pronounced. Governments that dare not ignore the threat of general annihilation in the nuclear weapons race hold endless conferences that fail to remove the threat because the parties will not accept supranational authority. Interventionary invasions contemptuous alike of legal rules and all notions of justice and humanity have reached an unprecedented scale. National claims to vast areas of ocean are enforced by the arrest of fishing vessels hundreds of miles from shore, while successive conferences draw up solemn proclamations declaring the ocean and its floor with their living and other resources a common heritage of mankind to be developed, conserved and distributed for the common good. Murder, kidnapping, hijacking and destruction by terrorist bands in the service of political factions are unrestrained because national interests will not submit to the necessary measures of control. Meanwhile, only 45 of the 144 states pledged by the UN Charter to the pacific settlement of disputes have agreed in advance to submit contested claims to the International Court of Justice, and many of these have whittled down their obligation by new restrictions. Canada's explicit rejection of the Court's authority to adjudicate in challenges to her control over a hundred miles of Arctic waters is only the most recent instance of this withdrawal into arbitrary discretion in a matter of general concern to the aggregate of states.

Such are the counter-currents against which every progressive internationalist movement must now struggle. That they have not put a dead stop to progress towards the rational administration of interests transcending national boundaries and capabilities is proof of the staying-power of reasoned idealism. Intergovernmental agencies still wrestle with such worldwide problems as economic development and distribution, health and welfare, pollution, protection and settlement of refugees, population and migration control, labor conditions, cultural interchange, and the protection of individual rights at home and abroad. Supplementing official effort in these directions, a growing complex of non-governmental associations is bringing together the liberal forces in many countries for united drives towards common objectives. Typical of these is the World Peace Through Law engaging the leaders of the legal profession in more than a hundred countries. Nor should we ignore the widespread activities of the world federalists. Their aims will not be achieved overnight, but they are contributing importantly to that political re-education without which states cannot be expected to merge in a world community.

There are also signs that the physical and moral agony of the long war in Indochina may have taught even some of the greater actors on the world stage the weakness and the folly of brute force as an instrument of policy.

4
Law in the Relations of States

For the purpose of this book, we shall ignore the debate whether law can properly be said to exist in an aggregate of entities acknowledging no overall governing authority, no agencies of final interpretation and adjudication and no machinery of undiscriminating enforcement. Admitting these obvious differences from the legal systems of contemporary states, we hope to demonstrate that a large body of law-like norms exercises substantial influence upon the decisionmakers who determine the foreign policy of states and direct their business abroad. Using the common terminology we shall call this "international law." We believe the demonstration important because there is a tendency in the recent behavioral study of international relations to neglect the role of law.

We do not acknowledge error in using analogies from the internal law of states (technically termed "municipal law"), though such analogies are condemned by some contemporary theorists.[1] We hold, for instance, that order is the prime function of law, and that order in the aggregate of states (which, without denying its inchoate character, we call "the world community") is the objective in the conscious formation of norms for the guidance of governments in their mutual relations. After summarizing what we believe to be the principal uses of law within the state, we shall therefore without apology identify corresponding uses of norms in the world community. We shall even attempt to establish that in the international sphere there is a difference, corresponding to that in the national sphere, in the operation and weight of ethical principles as compared with legal norms. Governments are apt to invoke law more than ethics in stating or rejecting claims. The comity

of nations is an ethical category and breaches of comity are less
seriously regarded than breaches of international law. In making
these comparisons, however, we do not argue, as some writers
do, that law in the international sphere has an influence upon
practice equal to its influence within the state.

What role does law play within the state? Law is:

(a) The constitution, that is to say the body of rules and principles,
written or unwritten, that define the purposes for which and the
ways in which the state's power is to be used, marking out the
boundaries of executive, judicial and legislative authority and prescribing the mode in which the agents of the state are selected;

(b) The most important part of the norms prescribing the conduct
of individuals and groups within the state's territory, prohibiting
acts injurious to the national values, defining the status, capacity,
rights and duties of persons, establishing forms of transactions, and
determining the distribution of property;

(c) The procedure in the courts where judges and juries confirm
or dismiss charges of crime, complaints of injuries (torts, delicts),
breaches of contract, and assess penalties;

(d) The orders, operations and proceedings of administrative agencies;

(e) The act of the policeman enforcing rules and executing judicial
decisions;

(f) The tax bill that exacts the wherewithal to pay for governmental
activities;

(g) The statutes and regulations imposing military and other
public duties.

How much of all that is to be found in the so-called family
of nations or world community?

Until the present century there was little in the way of international
or supranational constitution, though the concert of Europe may
be regarded as an early experiment in that direction. Since 1920
we have had the Covenant of the League of Nations and the
Charter of the United Nations, each purporting to be the constitution
of an international organization charged with the maintenance of
peace and the overall direction of agencies serving the common
welfare. Neither of these constitutions established judicial or legislative
authority over states, and the administrative authority of the specialized agencies was limited to specific functions and even then qualified
by the state's liberty of withdrawal.

Article 16 of the League Covenant embodied the first serious
plan for a standing agency to cope with breaches of the peace
by states. How it failed is a familiar story. The plan was taken

up and, on paper, strengthened in the United Nations Charter. Article 42 of the Charter went much farther than the Covenant had. Whereas the Covenant had empowered the League Council only to recommend, the Charter authorized the Security Council to "*take* [emphasis added] such action by air, sea or land forces as may be necessary to maintain or restore international peace and security." But how was this to be done? Only by the use of armed forces to be placed at the disposal of the Security Council in accordance with special agreements to be concluded between that body and each member of the UN. The Charter came into force thirty-one years ago, but Soviet opposition has prevented the conclusion of such agreements. The Security Council, for any military action that a majority may favour, is accordingly reduced to mere recommendation, and even that is subject to veto. Yet in spite of all these ostensibly unforeseen difficulties, which go far to neutralize the formal advance over the League, the UN has been able to put into the field military units that have substantially moderated the violence of the contending parties. Examples are the Military Observer Group in Kashmir, UNEF in the Suez crisis, and the UN operations in the Congo and in Cyprus.

The Korean war that began in 1950 is a special case, where the repulse of North Korea's invasion of the South was predominantly an enterprise of the United States and would probably have been undertaken even without the blessing of the UN. As it was, the United States did operate under the banner of the world organization and was assisted by minor contingents volunteered by other members. The mandate from the Security Council could never have been given but for the absence of the Soviet representative and the dubious assumption that in the circumstances the Council could legally act without the concurrent vote of one of its permanent members. When the Soviet representative resumed his seat, the General Assembly continued the action initiated by the Council, and the ease with which it commanded the necessary two-thirds vote left no doubt that the opposition to the combined efforts of North Korea, the Soviet Union and the Chinese People's Republic to conquer the peninsula expressed a strong majority will. The experience also demonstrated that the UN is not necessarily paralyzed when it has to proceed against the will of a permanent member of the Security Council. The Uniting for Peace Resolution of 1950, passed over Russian opposition, set the procedure for General Assembly peace-restoring action in a struggle where Britain and France were ranged against Egypt.

We have observed that the Charter failed to establish judicial authority. In this respect it went no further than the League Covenant. The new statute, like its predecessor, made provision for optional acceptance of the ICJ's jurisdiction in future disputes, but thus far considerably fewer than half the members of the UN have made the necessary declaration. The Soviet Union, though it has always had a judge in the Court, has stubbornly refused to submit disputes, and the United States still maintains the elastic Connally reservation of domestic jurisdiction.

Admitting all the difficulties of law enforcement now so manifest in long established nation-states, we submit that the existence there of courts with compulsory jurisdiction and enforcement agencies subject to no veto creates a degree of security, of predictability in relations and of confidence in legitimate expectations that is wanting in the international sphere. Residents in such states do not yet consider it necessary to arm against one another; the great majority still quietly count on getting what they have lawfully bargained for. We still have far to go before international law can do for its subjects what municipal law does for the persons and groups that live under it. But that is the aim of current development, and we are on our way.

Turning now from the obvious deficiencies of the international order, we shall examine some of the more important questions arising in the relations of states for which answers are officially sought in international law. The examination will show both how far the existing law of nations has been shaped by the theory and practice observable in municipal systems and how freely collective efforts to cope with new problems draw upon the same sources.[2] (The theory and practice to which we refer do not necessarily embody those "general principles of law, recognized by civilized nations" which Article 38 of the Statute of the ICJ instructs the Court to apply; what we have in mind are doctrines and institutions appearing with minor variations in different, but by no means necessarily all, systems. Of course this clause in the Statute is itself evidence of the reliance upon municipal analogies that we are attempting to demonstrate.)

I STATEHOOD

One primary question that the law of national communities must answer is: Who are their members? We shall presently see how the question is dealt with in municipal systems, but the answer offers little or no guidance in determining membership in the community of states. The fact that there was here no ready analogy perhaps explains why there is still so much debate about the connection between membership on the one hand and the existence and recognition of statehood on the other.

For the earliest writers, the law of nations (*jus naturale* and *jus gentium*) was world law equally binding upon governments and individuals. The sovereign and the common man were alike members of a world community and, in their different stations, subjects of its law. Even as late as the eighteenth century, when *jus gentium* was giving way to *jus inter gentes* and the dominant doctrine made states alone subjects of that law, the literature ignored the question how statehood and membership of the community of states was acquired, taking for granted an existing community of states living under "the public law of Europe" and equally entitled to its benefits. It was the positivism of the nineteenth century, operating in an expanding area of inter-governmental relationships, that produced the doctrine that statehood resulted from recognition by existing states, and there have been distinguished jurists of our time who have insisted that this is still the answer to our question.[3]

This constituent doctrine of recognition has the curious consequence that a community must be considered a state *vis-à-vis* those states that have recognized it and a non-state *vis-à-vis* all others. Another logical inference was that non-recognizing states owed no legal duty to the unrecognized community and were at liberty to treat it as they saw fit.

This was too barbarous a conclusion to win general approval, and an alternative was found in the doctrine that recognition was not constituent but only declaratory. The state came into existence when an independent community under a firmly established government had control, with a normal prospect of permanence, in a defined territory. These were the conditions of statehood, and recognition was nothing more than acknowledgment by other states that they had been met.

Practice today indicates that if an abstract rule on the matter can be said to exist, this is it. But how can it be applied with finality to specific cases? Governments may quite sincerely take different views as to the degree of control exercised by the administration claiming statehood, or as to the likelihood of its permanence. They may withhold recognition for purely political reasons, because they disapprove of the regime or wish to avoid offending a state from which the claimant community has recently broken off. Alternatively, they may grant premature recognition in order to encourage a regime that they favor. The absence of an authoritative judicial organ means that so basic a question as this may remain indefinitely unsettled.

Today, however, we have institutions that formally make statehood independent of recognition by individual states. The principle of self-determination enunciated in Article 1, paragraph 2 of the United Nations Charter cannot be reconciled with any right of individual states to deny statehood. More decisive still is Article 4, which means that admission to the United Nations is a certificate of statehood. These stipulations confirm our view that, save for internal purposes, recognition is a political act with no legal consequences.

State A may of course recognize state B, but refuse to recognize state B's present government, that is to say refuse to admit that that government is the legal agent of state B. Again this stance may result from genuine doubt of effective control, which is the proper criterion here, or from mere disapproval, or from deference to an earlier regime. The prolonged refusal of the United States to give explicit recognition to the government of the People's Republic of China was due partly to disapproval and partly to commitments to Taiwan. Like the recognition of states, the recognition of governments is a political act devoid of legal consequences outside the national forum. (Within the state, a government's refusal to recognize a state or its government may mean that the national courts will deny the validity of action taken by the unrecognized state or government affecting private rights.)

2 TERRITORY, SOVEREIGNTY AND JURISDICTION

Territory is defined by some jurists as the geographical area within which a state exercises its sovereignty. The definition has been criticized as a barren abstraction draining the national home of all its intensely emotional meaning.[4] It is, however, legally correct, and the question is immediately raised: How is this area determined?

The nearest thing to a general answer here is effective control maintained with the intention of permanency. The recognized modes of acquisition are clearly derived from the Roman law of immovable property—*occupatio*, the taking over and holding of land not belonging to any other state (*res nullius*); long, undisputed possession of land that had previously belonged to another state (*longi temporis possessio*); conquest, the military taking over of land from a defeated enemy who has given up all serious attempt to recover it; cession, the agreed transfer of land, for example in a treaty of peace, even where the transfer was imposed, the difference from conquest being the positive act of transmission as distinguished from tacit acquiescence. A very minor mode of acquisition, the shift of soil by alluvion from one bank of a boundary stream to the other, was an application of the Roman *accessio*. The long series of disputes between the United States and Mexico regarding the Rio Grande border demonstrates that a minor mode of territorial loss or gain may be a major source of dispute.

Acquisition by conquest of forced cession came under heavy attack after World War I. It was less than logical to outlaw war without outlawing territorial gains by war. The "Stimson doctrine" was contained in the note of 7 January 1932 from the United States to Japan and China informing those countries that Washington did "not intend to recognize any situation, treaty, or agreement which may be brought about by means contrary to the covenants and obligations of the Pact of Paris of August 27, 1928, to which treaty both China and Japan, as well as the United States, are parties." The effect of this was repeated in the note of twelve members of the Council of the League of Nations to Japan on 16 January 1932. In Article 2 of the Anti-War Treaty signed at Rio de Janeiro on 10 October 1933, the parties undertook not to "recognize any territorial arrangement which is not obtained by pacific means, nor the validity of the occupation or acquisition of territories that may be brought about by force of arms." (U.S. Treaty Series No. 9061.) In view of these precedents, it is somewhat surprising that there is no explicit undertaking of the sort in the United Nations Charter. Yet it is hardly conceivable that an impartial international tribunal, taking into account previous agreements and the Charter's provisions for the prevention or repression of the aggressive use of force, could admit title in a state that has forcefully taken over territory. It is our view that the rule is now part of the general international code.

As for the persons over whom jurisdiction may lawfully be exercised, the international code permits each state to determine who are its nationals. In some states the basic criterion is birth within the territory (*jus soli*); in others, it is parentage (*jus sanguinis*), that is to say the child takes the nationality of a parent, usually the father. Nowadays many states use both criteria. For example, under the law of the United States, which is primarily *jus soli*, the child born abroad of an American citizen is an American citizen.

Over its own nationals, the state has exclusive jurisdiction while they are in the national territory, and it may claim concurrent jurisdiction in regard to acts done by them abroad. It is also entitled to control the conduct of aliens within its territory, with certain exceptions, to be noted in Section 5 below in favor of the accredited representatives of foreign states.

Territory being regarded as a precious asset, the geographical lines dividing states are often in dispute, just as the boundaries of private landed property are the subject of much litigation in national courts. Frontier disputes have been the occasion for many international arbitrations and, just as national courts find guidance in national law, so international tribunals base their awards on norms such as those mentioned above, which they take to be generally accepted by states.

3 THE RESPONSIBILITIES OF STATES FOR DELICTS AND CRIMES

International law has long made states responsible for wrongs to
aliens as, for example, when they take over property without adequate
compensation, or fail to prevent personal injuries that could have
been prevented by efficient and unprejudiced police action. In such
cases the wronged alien must exhaust local remedies, that is to
say take any steps available under the local law to obtain redress.
If he is finally denied justice, he may then appeal to his own
state for action on his behalf. Since the early nineteenth century
there have been great numbers of inter-state arbitrations in such
cases, and a rich body of arbitral case-law has accumulated. Yet
the task of codifying this law has proved at least as difficult as
any legal formulation attempted since World War I. Differences
on the standard of justice to be applied in determining the responsibility of states defeated the Hague Codification Conference of 1930
and continue to delay the International Law Commission of the
United Nations. A further obstacle is the resistance of the communist
nations to the establishment of a rule of prompt and adequate
compensation to aliens whose property is included in a general
nationalization.

World War II stimulated a strong official movement to punish
on behalf of the community of states crimes against the peace
and security of mankind, war crimes, and violations of basic human
rights. The United Nations Security Council can and does impose
sanctions upon states held to be threatening peace. Further, the
victors in World War II set up international courts at Nuremberg
and Tokyo that imposed death sentences and lesser punishments
upon leaders in the governments and armed forces of the defeated
powers. Since it is not possible to hang or behead a state, and
barely possible to imprison one, the victorious powers relied upon
the new doctrine of personal responsibility for acts of state that
had been indecisively and unsuccessfully invoked after World War
I. At its 1946 session the UN General Assembly unanimously endorsed
the principles asserted by the prosecution at Nuremberg, and in
the following year it instructed the International Law Commission
to formulate them and draft a code of offenses against the peace
and security of mankind. In 1950 the ILC submitted its formulation
of the Nuremberg principles to the Assembly, which sent the text
to governments for their observations. The draft code of offenses
was submitted to the Assembly in 1951, but consideration of its
content has been repeatedly postponed pending a definition of aggres-

sion. For the same reason the statute of an international court drafted by a special committee of seventeen in 1953 still awaits Assembly deliberation. Since 1952 the Assembly has had special committees working on the problem of defining aggression, but as late as 1970 further time had to be granted for completion of the task.[5]

Dilatory as it is, the effort to establish criminal law and procedure for the world community testifies to a continuing demand for legal structure corresponding to that of the state.

4 TREATIES, CONTRACTS AND QUASI-LEGISLATION

The role of contract in modern life hardly needs elaboration. Within the state and across national boundaries contractual relationships are the web of domestic, social, economic and cultural organization and interchange. The counterpart in relations among states is the treaty, and the maxim *pacta sunt servanda* (agreements must be kept) is constantly cited as a basic tenet of international law.

But the treaty, besides serving the purpose of contract between states, is also our nearest approach to a legislative instrument in the international sphere. When a number of states wish to establish a new pattern of relationships, or to clear up debated points in a pattern established by usage, they resort to a multilateral "law-making" treaty. This is how international organizations have been set up, from the Universal Telegraph and Postal Unions of the mid-nineteenth century to the League of Nations and United Nations of the twentieth. It is also the mode of codification, as in the four Geneva Conventions of 1958 on the Law of the Sea.

There remains the great difference between this "quasi-legislation" and the statutes enacted by national parliaments that the former is binding only upon consenting states whereas national legislation binds irrespective of individual consent. This we believe true despite the Advisory Opinion handed down by the ICJ in 1948 on *Reparation of Injuries Suffered in the Service of the United Nations*, to the effect that the states that drew up the Charter, constituting as they did "the vast majority of the members of the international community" had the power to create "an entity possessing objective international personality, and not merely personality recognized by them alone." It can hardly be regarded as present international law that a conference, however numerous the states represented and however large the majority, can make law for states not present or not ratifying the decisions taken.

The treaty has long been the mode of codifying international law, witness those produced by the Congresses of Westphalia, 1648,

Utrecht, 1713, Vienna, 1815, and Paris, 1856, and by the Hague Peace Conferences of 1899 and 1907. With the rapid growth of "conference diplomacy" in this century, it has become also the chief mode of development. Compared with the slow and uncertain evolution of custom, it presents distinct advantages. The ratified document reduces uncertainties of meaning and of consent. To the newly independent states it offers a participation in the law-making process, the denial of which in the colonial era they cite in justification of their rejection of parts of the traditional body of norms.

There were, however, large areas of disagreement and uncertainty touching such questions as conference procedure; terminology; the point at which obligation began; the conditions of valid ratification; the effect of war, fundamental change of circumstances, special difficulty of performance, or breach by one party, upon treaty obligations; the validity of reservations; and the canons of interpretation. This explains the importance of the prolonged work of the International Law Commission culminating in 1969 at Vienna when the elaborate Convention on the Law of Treaties was drawn up. The text is in part codification and in part development, as indeed all "law-making" treaties are. It clarifies old principles and introduces new ones, and presents the world community with a greatly improved quasi-legislative process.

5 DIPLOMATIC AND CONSULAR INTERCHANGE

The earliest written history records the reciprocal grant of special protection for the envoys sent by one ruler to another, but it was not until the sixteenth and seventeenth centuries of our era that these scanty precedents began to be elaborated into a panoply of special rights and a broad immunity from civil and criminal law in the country of mission. As time went on the rules governing diplomatic relations were not only worked out in great detail; they were relatively well observed. Sovereigns and their agents prized the prestige and privilege of their status in foreign countries and these could be preserved only on condition of reciprocity. Failure in one country to live up to the pattern could be followed by easy retaliation upon its representatives abroad.

In our age of instantaneous communication, when no important decision need be taken without specific instruction from home, governments still attach great importance to diplomatic privileges and immunities. Moreover, the position of the consul who, as the historical protector of merchants and sailors in foreign parts, enjoyed little in the way of special status, has in recent years been increasingly assimilated to that of the diplomat. Here again, recent codification has removed differences and produced a clear and consistent body of norms. Conferences at Vienna in 1961 and 1963 adopted Conventions first on diplomatic and then on consular interchange and immunities. The fact that embassies and consulates are now in all countries hostages to demonstrating mobs and kidnapping terrorist bands has not led to any observable tendency to replace a grandiose, costly and vulnerable mode of representation with a system relying upon less adorned agents and the abundant mechanical methods of information and communication.

6 EXTRATERRITORIAL RIGHTS AND DUTIES, THE OCEANS, AIR SPACE, OUTER SPACE

The Roman legal concept of the sea was *res communis*, a domain subject to none and open to all (*Digest* 1.8.1; 1.8.2.1; *Institutes* 2.1.1). In the Middle Ages, practice ignored this maxim and large expanses of ocean were claimed by various states. By the end of the eighteenth century, the principle of freedom of the seas had regained its ascendancy, and the medieval claims were being reduced to assertions of exclusive authority in variously defined marginal belts and in "historic bays." Throughout the nineteenth century, the movement towards a regime that would clearly delimit national rights and community interests in the oceans becomes increasingly visible. Bilateral treaties and national legislation establishing rules that commended themselves to other governments, arbitral awards by distinguished international tribunals, and the persuasive treatises of learned publicists, all contributed to the development or hardening of rules on the outer limits of national jurisdiction, on rights of innocent passage through straits and territorial waters, on authority over ships, on safety of navigation, and on maritime fisheries.

Since the creation of the League of Nations in 1920, this haphazard approach to the regulation of a domain so important to the race as a whole has been succeeded by systematic collective development. The first step was taken when the law of the territorial sea was selected for codification at the Hague Conference of 1930. Six years of preparatory work by an international committee that sent out elaborate questionnaires to governments, and a month of negotiation at the Conference, failed to bring agreement on the central question of the width of the marginal belt. Yet the effort was not wasted. It revealed, as nothing had previously done, the vast

uncertainties of a normative system based upon the supposed consensus of states. It had been assumed that the three-mile norm,
with a few tolerated exceptions, had gained general acceptance.
The Conference discovered that a strong minority (which have since
become a majority) were unwilling to be bound by such a rule.
They denied having consented to it and demanded breadths up
to twelve miles. Since majorities cannot yet legislate for the world,[6]
there was, legally, no general three-mile limit.

The International Law Commission of the United Nations took
up the task of formulating a code not only for territorial waters,
but for the high seas, ocean fisheries, and the continental shelf.
The result was the four conventions on these subjects drawn up
at Geneva in 1958. These remove long-standing disagreements about
the passage of foreign private and public ships through territorial
waters; adopt a mathematical definition of bays and define the
limits of national sovereignty in them; establish rules on jurisdiction
over ships; chart a new regime for ocean fisheries, and formulate
principles to reconcile national rights of exploitation on the continental shelf with a general freedom of navigation.

Not content with this vigorous revision of sea law, the United
Nations is proceeding towards further implementation of the concept
of the oceans as public domain of a world community. On 17
December 1970, the General Assembly unanimously adopted Resolution 2749 (XXV) embodying a Declaration of Principles Governing
the Sea-Bed and the Ocean Floor. The area is declared to be
"the common heritage of mankind, subject to no state's sovereignty."
It is reserved for peaceful purposes and its resources are to be
developed, under rules and machinery to be established, for the
general benefit of the race. A further resolution of the same date
called for a conference in 1973 to define the regimes and set
up the necessary structure.[7]

We still lack a uniform limitation of the territorial belt. There
is nothing in the existing law of nations to prevent states from
claiming up to twelve miles; but the stipulation in the 1958 Convention on the Territorial Sea limiting the "contiguous zone" to twelve
miles may be interpreted as forbidding claims beyond that distance
from shore. That this is in process of becoming the general rule
limiting the territorial sea is attested by various recent developments.
One is its adoption as outer boundary of exclusively national fishing
waters by various countries, including the United States, that have
not yet formally abandoned the three-mile measure for general
purposes. Another is the Treaty Prohibiting the Emplacement of
Nuclear and Other Weapons of Mass Destruction, approved by
the General Assembly on 7 December 1970. The prohibition applies
only outside the twelve-mile zone.

Air space

The Paris Convention on Air Navigation, 1919, and the 1944 Chicago
Convention on International Civil Aviation provide an instructive
example of the way in which states now meet problems of general
concern posed by new technological developments. The military
uses of aircraft in World War I had revealed the peril to which
freedom of air navigation, corresponding to freedom of the seas,
would expose all nations. Any pre-war disposition to assimilate
air to ocean was abandoned, and the Paris Convention stipulated
complete sovereignty of each state in the air over its territory.
To secure the rights of passage that the prospective expansion
of commercial air navigation would demand, states had to become
parties to the Convention, and the text laid it down that the
parties should not admit aircraft of non-contracting states except
by special temporary permit. Bilateral agreements with non-contracting states providing for a general right of entry were not permitted
until 1926, when an amendment came into force. The establishment
of international airways required the consent of the states flown
over, even among parties to the Convention.

The International Commission for Air Navigation set up under
the Convention had the power to make and amend, by majority
vote, regulations on the licensing of aircraft and crews for international flights. It was charged with the exchange of information
regarding improvements in meteorology, communications and safety
equipment. It was replaced by the International Civil Aviation
Organization (ICAO) created by the Chicago Convention of 1944
on International Civil Aviation.

Like its predecessor, whose functions it took over, ICAO makes
majority decisions. It has, however, a greatly increased range of
authority. Subject to appeal to the International Court of Justice,
it adjudicates in disputes relating to the interpretation and application
of the Chicago Convention. It can apply effective sanctions such
as suspension of the voting rights, transit and landing rights of
delinquent states.

Apart from the creation of ICAO, the greatest advance made
at Chicago was the two-freedoms agreement that gave the parties
the right of transit for international airways and the liberty to
land for refuge from storms and other non-traffic purposes. The
right to discharge and pick up passengers and freight was the
subject of a so-called five-freedoms agreement, which was ratified
by no more than sixteen states, subsequently denounced by five.
For the most part, these traffic rights can still be obtained only
by special treaty.

ICAO has recently been grappling with the gravest problem

in its twenty-five year history—hijacking. Here, if ever, is a case for recognition of a crime against humanity punishable, like piracy, wherever the criminal can be apprehended. The stage now reached is a Convention adopted by a Conference of seventy-seven states at The Hague on 16 December 1970 providing for the severe punishment of hijackers in accordance with this principle.

Outer space

The latest technological development to which man has had to adapt his institutions is the navigation of outer space with its actual and potential consequences such as the accomplished landings on the moon and the contemplated visits to other planets. Though no agreement has yet been reached on the arithmetical elevation at which national air space ends and outer space begins, there appears to be a working consensus that anything in or beyond orbit around the earth is outside the territorial jurisdiction of any state. Space-craft and space-stations armed with weapons of mass destruction pose a threat at least as formidable as that of armed aircraft in the national air space, and the need for protective measures against this new peril is no less great than was the need that the Paris Convention of 1920 tried to meet. The mode adopted in 1920 was recognition of the state's sovereignty in its air space and explicit legalization of the state's control of entry to and activity in that space. But outer space is space recognized as being beyond national sovereignty. The ancient tag—*cujus est solum, ejus est usque ad coelum* (he who has dominion over the ground has dominion up to the sky) has no practical application in this context unless indeed sky be defined as the upper limit of national air space, wherever that is. No state can control activity in outer space save in relation to space-craft taking off from its own territory. Any general control must be exercised by or on mandate from the collectivity of states, and the organization necessary for it has yet to be devised. Meanwhile, however, abstract rules designed to govern human activity in outer space and on celestial bodies have been agreed to by a large number of states. Resolutions unanimously adopted by the General Assembly of the United Nations in 1961 and 1963 laid down the following principles:

(a) Exclusively peaceful use of space;
(b) No nuclear or other weapons of mass destruction to be put in orbit or stationed in outer space or on any celestial body;
(c) No celestial body to be appropriated by any state;
(d) Human activities in space to be subject to international law;
(e) Launching states to be responsible for damage done to aliens by their space-craft;

(f) Space-craft and crews landing in foreign territory to be returned to the launching country.

These principles have now been given the additional authority that the treaty form is supposed to impart. At London, Washington and Moscow on 27 January 1967 a treaty embodying them was signed under the title Principles Governing the Activities of States in the Exploration and Use of Outer Space including the Moon and other Celestial Bodies. This came into force on 10 October 1967 and has now[8] been accepted by seventy-one states, not including the Chinese People's Republic. Observation must depend, as in most international undertakings, upon the good will and good faith of the parties.

7 SELF-DEFENSE AND WAR

The modern state assumes a monopoly of force. The ancient remedy of self-help is replaced by official measures of compensation or retribution. Only in immediate self-defense may the individual legally resort to violence, and even then the action taken is subject to scrutiny by public authority to determine its necessity and proportionality.

Self-defense has always been explicitly or tacitly excepted in international undertakings not to go to war. The exception was tacit in the League Covenant and Kellogg Pact; it is explicit in the UN Charter.

The Charter was designed to create a monopoly of force in the Organization. Military force was to be permissible only on mandate from the UN or in individual or collective self-defense and, as in municipal systems, the validity of the plea of self-defense is subject to decision by collective authority (Article 51).

This ambitious plan has not totally failed. While the veto has prevented it from effectively controlling resort to force by the great powers, the UN, as we have seen, has been able in some degree to check even that. But the plea of self-defense has been exploited to justify a type of military action which is supplanting traditional war in the international power struggle.

States engaged in the struggle to preserve or expand their area of control no longer forcefully annex strategically desirable territory. They merely endeavor, by military intervention if necessary, to ensure that the government of such territory is in friendly and subservient hands. Familiar examples are the measures taken by the USSR in Hungary in 1956 and in Czechoslovakia twelve years later. In both cases the necessity of crushing subversive elements plotting for the West and of preventing a breach in the defense perimeter was cited in justification. The long-drawn out conflict in Indochina has the same essential features. There a great power, impelled by strategic calculations mingled with an intense hostility to communism, and pleading collective self-defense against aggression from North Vietnam, has thrown large military forces into the support of governments that owe more to that assistance than to popular choice. The result has been devastation of territory, slaughter of civilians, large military casualties, and the diversion of billions of dollars needed for social welfare at home.

If there is anything to be gained from this prolonged catastrophe, it is the lesson that vast military superiority cannot count upon vanquishing dedicated opposition, and recognition of the dire need for collective control of foreign intervention in civil strife. Initiated early enough in the interventionary process, such control may be feasible even with the existing machinery of the UN, which proved conspicuously useful in the case of the Dominican Republic in 1964–5. But the chances would be improved by a clear prohibition of unilateral intervention even at the request of an incumbent government. Such requests, which intervening governments cite as legalizing their action, may be obtained from factions owing their governmental role more to foreign support than to any national consensus. The resulting intervention may lead, as it did in Indochina, to counter-intervention that escalates the conflict to the dimensions of major war.

Human rights

Hardly second in importance, or in difficulty, to the long effort to control international violence, is the more recent movement to establish law and machinery for the collective protection of human rights. This proceeds partly by the assimilation of municipal systems along lines laid down in 1948 in the General Assembly's Universal Declaration of Human Rights, and partly through Conventions, usually under UN auspices, imposing obligations upon the states parties.

The most novel and striking feature of this development is that it aims to arm the individual with rights enforceable, under international supervision, not only against foreign states but against his own state as well. This is what makes governments slow to ratify the two Draft Covenants adopted by the General Assembly in 1966. Political leaders join in voluble endorsements of the principles formulated in these instruments, but are for the most part loath to expose their governments even to such far from coercive sanctions as those proposed in the Draft Covenant on Civil and Political

Rights.

Western Europe leads the world in the regionally collective protection of the individual against oppressive or discriminatory treatment by his own or a foreign government. Proceedings under the Rome Convention of 1950, which set up the European Commission and Court of Human Rights, are conducted with the utmost deliberation; but individual petitions are examined, some even reaching the Court, and governments found delinquent have in a number of cases been induced to change their laws, remit sentences and make restitution. The record, as was to be expected in a radical innovation, is one of cautious progress that may prove a pioneering guide for other regional organizations and, eventually, for a more effective universal structure. In its culmination the movement would make the individual a citizen of a world community and direct subject of its law.

Foreign aid

Foreign aid to industrially under-developed countries is a recent phenomenon in international relations. Among the factors accounting for the new practice, two stand out. One is the need in the richer nations for new and assured sources of raw materials; the other is the now general conviction that the widening gap between the poverty of the "South" and the riches of the "North" is incompatible with lasting peace and security. We believe that a third factor, not so commonly acknowledged, has been operating importantly in this context, namely a relaxation of man's ancient inhumanity to man, and an accompanying growth in the sense and practical expression of common human sympathy.

What is the relevance of foreign aid in a study of the development and operation of legal norms in the relations of states? There is no international rule requiring that any percentage of gross national product be earmarked for distribution among the developing countries. There is, however, a complex of governmental and intergovernmental agencies formulating and carrying out programs of foreign aid. These range from the Foreign Aid Administration of the United States, through joint enterprises like the Colombo Plan, to the United Nations Development Program and the International Bank for Reconstruction and Development with its offshoots. These cannot exact funds; their function is to administer funds voluntarily given. Their operations are nevertheless profoundly significant in the development of international law. They implement the recognition of world-community needs and their labors express and increase the sense of community which is the indispensable basis of law.

Environmental pollution

The same is true of the measures now being taken to control the pollution of the human environment. Here again is an only recently recognized threat to the life of mankind. And because the pollution of air, water and soil pays no heed to national boundaries, it has been quickly perceived as a problem calling for direct and effective international measures. This means new law and new administrative structure, and it is significant that the task has immediately been laid upon the UN. A UN Conference on the Human Environment was held in Stockholm in 1972.

CONCLUSION

We submit that the preceding record demonstrates the increasing use of juridical forms and methods in the efforts to cope with international problems, and a continuing reliance upon national legislative, administrative and judicial models in devising solutions. There is as yet no general willingness to follow the municipal analogy to its logical conclusion of overall authority, and no unified world government appears above our horizon. What we see is a persistent movement in that direction. Thus far the participants hungrily seek the efficiency of centralized direction but refuse to pay the price in terms of national sovereignty. The municipal analogy is counterproductive only when it encourages expectations that ignore the inevitable uncertainties of a political system without centralized power.

5
The Behavioral Sciences in the Study of Conflict

No account of theoretical attempts to explain the phenomena of international politics can be thought even partially adequate unless it takes into account the behavioral approach to the subject. There are, of course, enormous differences of opinion about exactly what the term "behavioral" means with the result that supporters and opponents of the movement all too often are engaged in a dispute about the meaning of words with the end product consisting largely of a sophisticated muddle in which key issues are blurred or even lost altogether. Excessive claims are made—"all segments of political science can be treated behaviorally"[1]—which in turn call forth sharp rebuttals and denials.[2] It is all great fun for the participants but when the smoke of battle has cleared away, exactly what has been learned?

The answer one gives to this question will depend almost entirely on how broadly or how narrowly the issues are defined. If for example one begins by defining behavioral explanations as involving individuals rather than groups as the proper units for analysis, as excluding normative approaches and including regularities but never particular occurrences,[3] it is easy to show that the approach leaves out significant aspects of politics which interest most students of the subject. If, on the other hand, one lists the assumptions of the behavioral approach as involving "empirical observations" which are "systematic, visible, explicit, and reproducible,"[4] then any attack must, in effect, challenge the validity of scientific method, a difficult task indeed. A careful perusal of a recent summary of research findings reveals the interesting fact that analysts have studied groups as well as individuals (and at many levels from individual statesmen to the global system), have described individual events as well as observed regularities and included value studies among their concerns.[5] Hence one set of objections is revealed as nothing more than an arbitrary use of definitions for polemical purposes. It is true, and will always remain true, that if we define an approach so as to exclude important subjects germane to an inquiry, that approach will be (by definition) deficient. If, however, we include all pertinent matters, the question of whether an approach is valid or fruitful tends to become a function of the adequacy of the data available and the ingenuity of the theorist. Nor is it necessary to demand, as Easton seems to do,[6] a genuine synthesis of social science disciplines bringing together generalizations concerning fundamental units of analysis. This demand is premature and too ambitious for our present state of knowledge. Rather, the demand should be that sources are specified and that the data used be explicit, systematic and reproducible. No more is required and surely no less.

If this modest proposal is taken as a starting point—we can ask a more specific question: "In what ways can the behavioral sciences contribute to a study of international politics?" First, it is vital to make clear what they *cannot* do. They cannot provide a total approach to the subject. They can never *be* the study of international politics which occurs within particular structures under particular conditions.[7] They can, however, "contribute once relevant points of application have been identified."[8] The key questions then are posed, not in terms of absolutes, but rather in terms of what kinds of relevance such subjects have and what the limits of relevance are for the study of international politics. In short, what can we learn from them and how do they help us explain the phenomena?[9] A specific answer for social psychology is that it can contribute directly to the study of public opinion in the foreign policy process, it can aid in studying individual decision-makers, it can provide concepts for the study of the processes of negotiation and decision-making and it can aid in an examination of the assumptions of theory building and policy recommendations.[10]

If we look at some of the issues raised by social psychologists who have tried to apply their knowledge to international politics we find the following: aware that public opinion on foreign policy is a compound of ignorance and apathy, scholars go on to discriminate among *effective* public opinion, attempts to manipulate opinion, constraints perceived by the decision-makers and so on. In short, they move to delimit the study of opinion formation and its impact on decision-making. In the study of individuals, they do not fall into the trap of equating decision-making with the idiosyncratic behavior of individuals but rather they place such persons in the context of the roles which they play in the machinery of state, the images and motives which are national or elitist or personal in character and, in the process, throw light on the context and processes within which decisions are made.[11] Thus the analysis is as much concerned with behavior in terms of roles as it is with the behavior of persons and eliminates the superficial critique that such studies either reify the state or deal only with unique individuals. In fact they deal both with the structured nature of behavior (and hence the constraints on freedom of action) as well as with the distinctive type of behavior that occurs in the special circumstances which provide freedom of action in cases of vital national interest.[12]

A good deal of legitimate criticism of the uses to which behavioral studies are often put relates to the indiscriminate employment of experimental findings. These criticisms apply not only to experiments on interpersonal and intergroup relations but also to efforts to reproduce in the laboratory some of the basic conditions of international relations.[13] It is pointed out that a sharp difference exists between laboratory conditions and real-life situations, that participants in simulated studies are often students with no experience of actual decision-making dealing with make-believe stakes and that the results, therefore, are useless.[14]

Like much of life, these criticisms tend to be valid in what they affirm but less reliable in what they deny. The key issues in evaluating the experimental approach would seem to be the following: Has the experimenter isolated the crucial variables which govern the relationship in question? If so, does the experiment incorporate the important conditions of the situation which affect the factors being studied?[15] No general answer can be given to these two questions. Each experiment has to be evaluated in light of them and this means, among other things, that *only cooperative work is likely to prove fruitful in this area of research* since the evaluation and testing of experiments requires expert knowledge of both international relations and social psychology. More important, no laboratory results can have universal validity but rather each generalization must be "reexamined for each specific problem."[16] This means, in effect, that experimental results can be used to generate hypotheses in a given area of research if and only if significant variables are identified, if crucial conditions are reproduced and if results are tested in the real world and results are integrated with more general research. Needless to say very few studies meet these demanding conditions. Every article describing experiments designed for application in international relations should bear the inscription "use with care and caution."

These admonitions, however, are not meant to disparage or discourage the application of theories and hypotheses generated in behavioral studies to international relations. They are intended to warn against direct application in cases which presumably pose dangers of sharply different conditions. Nor should advocates of more traditional approaches rejoice concerning the difficulties described herein since their own work is subject to exactly the same limitations. They too must make assumptions about psychological processes, whether about individuals or about policies. All too often they put forward mere analogies as if they were general models and generalize airily across decades of time in a manner which ignores radically changed conditions.[17] In short, no matter what approach is used, the same problems of constructing demonstrable knowledge remain.

It will be realized at once that the issues posed by the application of behavioral science findings to international relations go to the very foundations of philosophy—to the nature of truth itself. The methods of the behavioral sciences must ultimately stand or fall by a basically pragmatic test: Do they attain their intended purposes of explaining, predicting and controlling the world?[18] In evaluating their claims to do so we must remember that their propositions are only *plausible*, not certain, *tentatively* acceptable in the light of the evidence and ultimately *defeasible*.[19] If these criteria are kept in mind we can offer a modest "yes, they help us to some degree, particularly since they remind us that much of what passes for knowledge is mere speculation and therefore should be treated with caution, particularly when such speculations form the basis for decisions which seriously affect the lives of ordinary citizens."

It is vital to grasp the fact that evaluation of empirical studies in behavioral science requires an intimate knowledge and study of the materials discussed in the literature. General collections of propositions are not likely to prove of much use, consisting as they do of a bewildering variety of hypotheses at different levels of analysis with little or no effort being made to clarify the behavioral assumptions on which the hypotheses rest.[20]

Some idea of the very real difficulties which lie in the path of applying empirical studies to problems in international relations will be revealed if we examine in detail work which has been done in the area of decision-making under conditions of uncertainty. This is an area of great potential interest to students of international politics, particularly that part of it which deals with risk-taking behavior since it is obvious that statesmen do take decisions which involve risks. Hence if studies revealed any patterns of risk-taking behavior in typical situations, a good deal of light might be thrown on a variety of important political activities.[21]

In this general area pioneer work was done by Ward Edwards[22] who conducted experiments on preferences among choices which differed in the probability of winning. His models assumed that a gambler will choose a bet with the maximum value and that this alternative can be calculated by multiplying the value of each outcome by the probability that the outcome will occur and summing these products over all outcomes. Among his findings was the fact that subjects had definite preferences for betting at some probability levels rather than others. Thus, at first blush, there appeared to be a certain measure of stability in what might be called a psychological scale of probabilities, a scale which did not correspond to a strict mathematical concept of probability.

Other experiments showed that psychological probability exceeded mathematical (i.e., statistical) probability at low values and is exceeded by the latter at high values. The findings applied to sophisticated people familiar with the mathematical theory of probability as well as naive subjects.[23] Hence, subjects did not maximize utility since no matter what the size of the prize they paid for prizes with small probabilities too generously and took prizes with large probabilities as bargains.

If additional experiments repeating Edwards' test had confirmed his findings, the hopeful student of international politics could have gone happily away to see if he could discover similar patterns in international decisions. Unfortunately the waters were muddied by other persons who tested Edwards' models for successful prediction with only moderate success.[24] Other scholars argued that, in addition to probability preferences, people's attitudes to risk involved what is called variance preferences—that is the amount of deviation in outcomes from the average amount obtained by betting. For example, an even money bet of five dollars and one at one dollar both have an expected value of zero but the potential losses are different in the two cases. In a series of tests Edwards[25] found shifts in preferences among bets which could be attributed to the variance factor. Once again a potentially clarifying result was blurred when the experiments were repeated with very different results. Slovic found that, while some persons had shifts in preferences which corresponded to Edwards' findings, others had preferences which were stable at different probability levels while still others had probability preferences which shifted systematically as the variance of the bets changed.[26] Results, therefore, were inconsistent with no clear-cut hypothesis explaining the relation between probability preferences and high risk-taking. In short, observations of choices did not distinguish the extent to which risk-taking was determined by individual differences in the *perception* of risk or by differences in the *reaction* to that perceived risk.[27] A similar problem confronts anyone trying to explain the reactions of Kennedy and Khrushchev in the Cuban Missile Crisis and much the same conclusion emerges.

The evidence does not permit us to specify unequivocally whether the decisions taken turned on the perception of or the reaction to perceived risks, let alone in exactly what manner and proportion. The truth is that risk is a concept with many dimensions. No one has fully explored that part of it which deals with preferences involving expected value, variance and probability in the precise sense that all three variables have been manipulated in a systematic manner.[28] Results are inconsistent at least in part because the measures used tap different dimensions of the behavior and because the experiments tried are often too crude to cope with the facts. If this applies to the relatively simple experiments surveyed, how much more difficult it would be to structure into the laboratory situation the kind of fear which must be present when decisions are taken in a great crisis involving the potential use of nuclear weapons. Clearly one's estimate of risk must be affected by the level of fear involved and this latter in turn must be related in some fashion to the probabilities of miscalculation and the magnitude of the disaster which would occur if such weapons were ever used.[29]

Some conception of the distance between the experimental results obtained in the above literature and the real world of international politics can be glimpsed if we now examine a theory of risk-taking derived from an actual study of several major crises.[30]

Let us now turn to the actual course of history and ask whether various crises show similar or different patterns in particular periods of history, what precisely the similarities or differences are, and, whether, for convenience, they can be ordered into a useful typology.

It should be said at once that the choice of crisis periods and of the factors selected as crucial will be decisive for the fruitfulness of the analysis. Bell, for example, regards the inter-war and post-war periods as comparable on the ground that the essential factors—the nature of the decision-makers, the communication between them, and the means available to make decisions effective—were not widely different in the two periods.[31] On the very face of it, this comparison seems odd since one would have thought significant differences existed between the two eras in terms of two of the criteria she selects. Certainly no risk-taker comparable to Hitler has emerged on the international scene as yet, and although communications may not differ all that much, the variation in means available does differ enormously. Bell attempts to get around this discrepancy by drawing a strained analogy between the present fear of nuclear war and the inter-war concern about the potential devastation available through conventional bombing.

Her analysis thus slides over some of the key differences in the two periods. The differences center around the speed, scale and certainty of the destruction available to decision-makers and amount to a radical change in the nature of deterrence. It was possible to argue, in the inter-war period, that while the costs of war would be very great indeed, the gains from war would produce a balance of advantage. Hence, everything turned on whether a significant lead in military capabilities could be exploited first diplomatically and then in the crucible of battle itself. In the conduct of crises, this meant that deterrence was ineffective relative to the superior side and crisis management was virtually a synonym for surrender. In short, superior capabilities could be translated into political gains; whereas, in the nuclear era, the strength of deterrent forces tends to produce conditions of stalemate. Deterrence cannot, except under special conditions, be used as a compellent.

Further, when Bell argues that identical weight has been given by decision-makers to the penalties of war throughout the post-1945 period, one feels that important distinctions between crises have been blurred. We would argue, on the contrary, that symmetrical expectations on penalties existed only in the period from the Cuban Missile Crisis to the present. In the 1945–53 period, the United States had a monopoly of both the nuclear bomb and the means of its delivery and hence American decision-makers could and did feel that, in a grave crisis, they held the high cards. This effect operated throughout the 1953–62 period and may even have played a critical role in the Cuban Missile Crisis itself. Symmetrical expectations do become important in the age of mutual deterrence but only as between parties with substantial second-strike capabilities.

All this indicates that we are unlikely to discover general patterns and regularities which can be applied to crises regardless of the time frame in which they occur. Rather, we must look for limited patterns, transitory regularities, which are temporarily restricted within definite bounds.[32] The most fruitful approach will be to regard risk-taking as the central focus with military capability as the key factor in deterrence. Hence, the major time division for purposes of comparison should be between pre-nuclear and nuclear crises, with a further subdivision based on the relative capabilities of the parties.

With the above time-frame in mind, let us look at crises as essentially competitions in risk-taking. The key question, then, becomes: "What determines the attitude of the powers towards risks?" Our answer will be that attitudes to risk will vary with the interplay of two factors—the relative military capabilities of the parties and the relative size of the stakes at issue for them. It is the *combination* of capabilities and the size of stakes which determines both *commitments* and the *severity* of the particular crisis. In order to trace the *outcomes* or *results*, it is necessary to compare the two sets of capabilities and stakes which represent the positions of the parties to the conflict.

The concept of military capabilities presents few difficulties for the analyst, whereas the notion of "stakes" poses a potential stumbling block. In order to avoid purely subjective judgments, our suggestion is that we make use of the insights of earlier analysts and base our classification of stakes upon the hierarchical structure of the international system.[33] The result would be a broad classification of stakes according to their estimated impact upon the rank of the state within the world hierarchy. Three broad categories then suggest themselves—survival stakes, landslide stakes (i.e., stakes which pose the danger of a hierarchical shift), and marginal stakes (stakes which pose the possibility of gains or losses but which do not involve a hierarchical shift). Thus, we would have a continuum of stakes calculated in terms of the estimated gain or loss in the hierarchy, and hence a propensity for risk-taking which would be directly proportionate to the value of the stakes at issue.

The diagram on page 57 presents the positions of the parties in four actual crises—Hungary, Cuba, Formosa Straits and Lebanon—in order to illustrate the essentials of the argument. In particular, it is important to stress the fact that it is the *combination* of capabilities and stakes and the *comparison* of these which explains the attitudes of the powers to risks and hence ultimately to the scope of their commitments, the severity of a crisis and, finally, to outcomes. Thus, in the case of Hungary, the Soviet Union confronted a situation which could have led to the spreading collapse of its East European sphere of influence and felt able to use its superior conventional power to crush the revolution even though it suffered from an inferior nuclear position. The United States, on the other hand, had a severe conventional inferiority partly due to geographic factors and, because of its marginal stake, could not issue credible nuclear threats.

The Cuban Missile Crisis was, in effect, a Hungary in reverse with the United States having the largest stake, overwhelming conventional capabilities in the area of conflict and a nuclear superiority to boot. It therefore felt free to issue a threat of massive retaliation and confront the Soviets with a choice between retreat, a nuclear confrontation or initiation of a crisis in some area where the Soviet Union had a clear advantage. In order to pursue their policy to a successful conclusion the Soviets confronted choices which involved a threat to their survival or, at the very least, a potential hierarchical shift of position. In point of fact, they had only marginal stakes in the crisis and hence their propensity to take risks was reduced correspondingly in the crucible of decision.

In the two Formosa Straits crises (1954–5 and 1958), the United States had only marginal stakes but it enjoyed command of the

Positions of the Parties in Four International Crises

Military Capabilities	Marginal Stakes	Landslide Stakes	Survival Stakes
Nuclear superiority	1 *Hungary*—United States 3 *Formosa Straits*—United States 4 *Lebanon*—United States	2 *Cuba*—United States	
Nuclear inferiority	2 *Cuba*—Soviet Union 3 *Formosa Straits*—Communist China 4 *Lebanon*—Soviet Union	1 *Hungary*—Soviet Union	
Conventional superiority	3 *Formosa Straits*—United States 4 *Lebanon*—United States	1 *Hungary*—Soviet Union 2 *Cuba*—United States	
Conventional inferiority	1 *Hungary*—United States 2 *Cuba*—Soviet Union 3 *Formosa Straits*—Communist China 4 *Lebanon*—Soviet Union		

sea and air and it confronted, in China, an opponent with no nuclear weapons. Hence the United States could manipulate the risk levels at will. In the extremities of the crisis, it could and did make nuclear threats, with the Soviet Union entering the arena only when the situation had passed the danger point.

Lebanon was the least dangerous of the crises listed, with marginal stakes for all the parties and a complete Soviet inability to bring its conventional military power to bear.

The typology also helps us understand why parity in nuclear

weapons became a major Soviet objective (and explains perhaps their decision to put intermediate range ballistic missiles in Cuba in the first place); why, as the era of mutual deterrence loomed ahead, the United States began to stress the importance of "flexible response" (an elaborate term for increased conventional military capacity); and finally, why the brinkmanship of Foster Dulles disappeared as a standard operating procedure.

The above analysis should not lead us to believe that crises can be rendered stable by the application of doctrines of crisis management. For the analysis strongly suggests that crisis stability may have been a passing phenomenon due largely to American nuclear preponderance and, above all, to the fact that no crisis arose in issues where vital interests were involved for *both* competitors. What appears to have been superior crisis management may really have been nothing of the sort, but rather the relative ease with which one great power or the other could manipulate a position of superiority. In short, we may yet experience extremely dangerous crises in the new era of mutual deterrence.

If the above analysis is correct in its basic outlines, we can predict the types of crises which would be most dangerous and unstable. The most serious of all would be a situation which combines nuclear parity, equality of stakes involving a potential hierarchical shift and an advantage in conventional military power for the state which wishes to change the existing distribution of power. A miscalculation in such circumstances could be fatal either because of an underestimation of the value of the stakes at issue or because the defending side gambled on the restraining power of a threat of mutual suicide in order to prevent a loss of position.

Thus, while the range of stakes for which states will knowingly risk nuclear war has become more circumscribed and states have sought to minimize dangers by reliance on conventional military capabilities, they show few signs of changing in a fundamental manner the game itself. This may be because the crises they have experienced have not seemed dangerous enough to warrant the radical changes necessary to transform the risky environment in which they live. So far they have relied on unilateral measures to reduce the vulnerability of their strategic weapons, more direct communications and a partial check to the nuclear arms race. These are only stop-gap measures. Sooner or later states will have to face the prospect of extensive arms control and disarmament. Let us hope that this course will be adopted before and not after the tragic events which could ensue as the result of a great crisis.

The above theory of crises has been cited at some length in order to show the rather sharp differences which exist between such an empirical theory and the laboratory experiments on risk-taking. The case studies are linked by a set of hypotheses derived directly from empirical facts, not from laboratory experiments. They argue that attitudes to risk are based on the size of the stakes at issue and the military capabilities of the parties. The list of crucial conditions is described as involving a pre-nuclear and nuclear time period with the model predicting behavior under conditions of nuclear symmetry. Thus, the nature of risks and stakes and the resources open to the parties differs markedly from the basic conditions of the laboratory and it is very difficult to see how they could be duplicated in an experiment. This does not mean, however, that helpful insights might not be gained in theory-building by using behavioral techniques as a supplement to and a check on the model proposed. For example, it would be most interesting and enlightening if a group of simulation experiments were devised to test the validity of the model both in terms of its own internal consistency and in terms of modifications suggested by the response of subjects. It is evident that any such experiment would gain in reality if participants in the first instance were experienced decision-makers familiar with the uses and effects of weapons. Their responses could be checked over the whole range of the model and then compared with results based on the responses of naive subjects whose expertise was minimal. One suspects that a reasonably good test of the model's general accuracy would be obtained and some more or less severe changes indicated by the pattern of replies. Conflicts between the theory and the simulation could then be dealt with by reviewing the basic historical data for new evidence in the light of discrepancies, refining the model accordingly or, perhaps, abandoning it completely for a better model suggested to the experimenters in the light of the simulation. It is in some such interplay between real world models and laboratory tests that many of the contributions of the behavioral sciences can best be realized.[34]

An equally interesting source for the generation of hypotheses and their testing would be to compare state behavior with the behavior of gangs in a field situation. Even a tentative look at one major study of gangs reveals some startling similarities in the two sets of behavior.[35] A gang, like a nation state, is a conflict group which develops through strife and thrives on warfare; its status is maintained through fighting; it defends or attacks territory; fears intervention by third parties; engages in cycles of conflict and accommodation; forms alliances and federations; enters into treaties of peace and so on. Both groups are engaged in a struggle for survival in a hostile world and are caught up in the quest for power with a drive to dominate and manipulate others. It is difficult to believe that a cooperative study comparing and contrasting the behavior of these two groups would not reveal a great deal of interest particularly in how crises develop, subside or escalate into open war, the specific conditions which lead to negotiations and settlement, the part played in conflict by considerations of prestige and status and, finally, as a test of differing theories of conflict resolution.

Behavioral studies can make a contribution at a different level entirely from any mentioned thus far. We refer to a host of studies on the nature of aggression[36] dealt with by ethnologists, psychologists, sociologists and anthropologists. These attempt to get at the roots of behavior, to understand and analyze those aspects of experience which trigger, increase or diminish aggression.

These findings are of peculiar relevance because they go to the heart of the question whether human aggression is somehow a part of our animal ancestry and therefore in some sense inevitable. Lorenz argues that aggression is a product of natural selection, that it is spontaneous in the sense that it results from internal drives which must find expression. As such, it is virtually unmodifiable. His critics[37] accuse Lorenz of using biased examples, of misinterpreting the evidence, of drawing false parallels between animals and man and of using a false dichotomy between behavior which is genetically determined and behavior which is derived from experience. The latter point is of great importance for it poses the issue as to the extent to which genetic endowment or the environment is responsible for differences which exist between individuals or between species.[38]

The present state of our knowledge does not apparently permit a clear, unequivocal answer to this last question. For one thing ethnologists keep telling us that no two species behave alike.[39] For another, it is very difficult to distinguish between variables within the animal and variables in the environment. No generally accepted conclusions are available for basic questions such as: Is readiness to attack constant or variable? Could fighting be reduced by reducing population density or provocative stimuli? Tinberger points out that animals do avoid bloodshed. Aggression rarely occurs in a pure form but is one of two aspects of adaptive behavior. For example, members of a territorial species divide available living space after which they attack intruders but outside its home range the species withdraws when it meets an established owner.[40] Tinberger is inclined to believe that man still carries within him the animal heritage of group territoriality which cannot be eliminated by different ways of upbringing. If this is so, it is obvious that our historical experience has reinforced this behavior since all living space is divided on national and tribal lines. The issue then comes down to whether the behavior associated with group territoriality can be modified sufficiently to permit human survival in an age when "attack" involves the potential use of weapons of mass destruction. The question is of transcendent importance in that if man's ability to adjust his behavior is completely outpaced by historically determined changes in his environment (particularly the population explosion and the development of weapons), the chances for human survival are extremely small.

Anthropologists, while not denying the survival value of aggression in terms of the functions of spacing out populations, selection of the fittest mates for propagation and protection against predators, argue that we should begin with the patterns of violent behavior formed by culture.[41] In this view man is a domesticated caged animal in the sense that he is confined by nature and culture. He does have biologically learned propensities toward aggression but he differs in important ways from other animals. For example, he is not protected by instinctive responses which terminate ritual battles. More important he has a choice of viewing other men as being of the same species or as predators or prey. While it is true that no wild species displays the savagery of man in feuds, blood vengeance or torture, it remains the case that man can alter his cultural cage and regard other men as brothers entitled to protection. In short, man can restructure his culturally elaborated categories including the concept of war.

For the anthropologist war is a cultural invention which involves the social sanctioning of killing members of an opposing group. It does not have a specific biological base independent of culture. Rather, it is a functional response to a variety of identifiable conditions. All the evidence from anthropology suggests that a functioning invention will be used until rendered obsolete by another invention, by the disappearance of the function it performed or by becoming itself disfunctional. The question whether war has reached this latter point or not becomes at this juncture a matter for statesmen and peoples to decide. If the answer is "yes"—as it surely must be on any objective analysis of the evidence—we are left with the problems of how best to modify violence in the short run and finally how to eliminate it from intergroup relations.[42]

Once again we will find that the behavioral sciences can be of considerable assistance in approaching these tasks. Only a few examples will be cited but they will indicate the usefulness of a multidisciplinary approach both in terms of a division of labor and the advantages to be gained from cross-fertilization through new ideas and concepts. A broad eclecticism is the best recommendation in these areas as in the studies previously referred to.

One of the most provocative and interesting developments in recent work has been an emphasis on controlled communication as a technique of conflict resolution.[43] The argument is that there has been a progression in the modern world from direct judgment and enforcement to methods which draw on the points of view of the parties by techniques which inject new information concerning perception, escalation, interpretation, assessment of values and costs in a manner designed to assist in conflict settlement.[44] This view challenges the traditional realist view of international politics as based on state relations—the so-called "billiard ball" model—and the assumptions about conflict upon which it rests. In particular it challenges the view that international society is in a state of anarchy in which conflicts can only be settled or contained within a framework of threats and violence.[45] Hence legal rules as a restraint on aggression and intervention, sanctions enforced by law, arbitration, the control of conflicts by great powers or by supranational institutions are described as deficient methods or even as contributing to conflict. Instead, this view argues that conflict is a subjective condition and that resolution of conflict is possible by non-coercive means.

The assumption which underlies controlled communication is that conflict is a subjective phenomenon which occurs when accurate assessment of costs and values is prevented, rather than a process produced by aggressive tendencies determined by power relations.[46] Aggressive behavior is the result of a faulty appraisal of the total situation based on misperception by the parties in which distortion, negative feedback, reinforcement and so on rigidify the conflict. What is required is to transform a power relationship into a problem-solving one. To do this the following procedures are crucial: Each step must be fully under control of the parties with no obligation to accept settlement in advance; the role of third parties is to explain conflict in terms of origins, to expose the misperceptions which exist and to provide an accurate assessment of the costs of conflict relative to the goals sought. The conflict should be broken down into sub-disputes and, if necessary, according to the various factions involved. A key principle, therefore, is to resolve the conflict at local levels. Felt needs of the parties provide the framework for the exploration of possible solutions.

Basically, the aim is to move toward areas of functional cooperation which then provides the conditions for negotiations between the parties. Thus structural and institutional changes proceed from the level of the greatest transactions and are not imposed from the top.

At a world level the argument is that the billiard ball model promotes the status of authorities at the price of inhibiting political and social change by means of restrictive intervention through a threat system. Controlled communication on the other hand is based on the trends in world society which emphasize interdependence, smaller, non-aligned political units and the growth of functional institutions. In sum, the new approach looks toward the transformation of conflict into problem-solving based on the need to assist and adjust to change.

How are we to assess the basic validity of this contribution to conflict resolution? A number of ideas suggest themselves at the outset. Undoubtedly our perceptions of reality do tend to create the reality which they attempt to describe. If we perceive a world of hostile and aggressive states we tend to behave accordingly, finding it necessary to create threat structures in the shape of weapons and alliances to deal with these evils. But it does seem to be playing with words to assert that such perceptions are entirely misconceived. Studies of perception do show that people treat inputs from the environment in ways which involve the application of concepts to the data and the way the mind conceptualizes is determined in part by what has resulted from past interaction. This is then modified by failures in payoff when interacting with the world.[47] Who is to decide whether a particular model, which has been developed on the basis of such a process, is a more rational inference from the data of experience than another? From a strictly scientific standpoint Burton's model of perception is no more and no less subjective than the billiard ball model which he rejects. Where then can we turn for analytical help? While it is true that no political facts exist independently of our perception of them, the achievement of independent criteria to determine the *extent* of our misperception is no easy task. Earlier in this chapter we suggested that the practical test should be the success of theory in the effective guidance of action in the light of a governing purpose. That is to say, the test will be which model is more conducive to the achievement of the practical objective—in this case conflict resolution. By this test Burton's model would seem to be far and away the better adapted to existing conditions. There is a great deal of empirical evidence to support his major contention that intense conflict impairs perception and communication, that it limits the capacities of the parties for profound creative solutions, that competent and trustworthy third parties are necessary to illuminate the conflict, establish ground rules and suggest alternative solutions.[48]

If, however, the practical objective is not simply to resolve conflict but to resolve it on one's own terms, or, if one's objective is to expand one's position of power and influence through coercive techniques, then Burton's model fails lamentably. Indeed, he is to be found in the company of Woodrow Wilson who argued the Burtonian thesis a long time ago. "Peace," Wilson said, "could be secured if issues were settled not by diplomats or politicians eager to serve their own interests but by dispassionate scientists—geographers, ethnologists, economists—who had made studies of the problems involved."[49] The world has really made very little progress toward Wilson's goal in the intervening period. Some of this lack of progress can no doubt be attributed directly to misperceptions of the sort which Burton describes. A good deal of it, however, is due to other causes altogether, particularly the insistence of men and groups that power and favorable circumstances should be used for selfish purposes and to gain maximum advantages. This is no doubt wrong-headed and in today's world extremely short-sighted. It is also a fact about the nature of reality and as long as it is so there will be room for diplomacy based on pressure and threats and men will continue to rely at least in part on the uses of violence.

Both theory and reality, however, combine in the study of conflict to warn us that the old ways are becoming increasingly outmoded. Science, technology and nuclear weapons all point in the direction of functional obsolescence for the organized violence we call war. Burton and the behavioral sciences point us toward the future, to a world as yet unborn when the arts of conflict-resolution and problem-solving are taken seriously by men and nations.

6
Systems Theory: New and Old

Any text in the field of international relations makes constant but usually unsystematic use of the concept of "system." References are made to the "international system," the "global system," the "nation-state system," and so on often without clearly differentiating between the different uses of these terms. It seems the better part of wisdom, therefore, to examine the concept with care not merely because of the frequency with which it is abused but also because the scholarly literature' on systems theory has spawned an ever-proliferating body of complex jargon, contradictory assertions and, in general, considerable theoretical confusion. Such a process is all too familiar to students in the social sciences. Debates first produce excitement, then anger but little enlightenment and finally, through the sheer weight of the boredom and weariness evidenced in participants and bystanders alike, fruitful ideas are lost for long periods of time. Meanwhile, precious time and energy have been lost.

It seems sensible to begin with a few of the basic ideas involved in systems theory, attempting to set out the main objections and drawing some modest conclusions concerning the value of the various approaches. We begin, therefore, with some remarks on General Systems Theory, go on to a short examination of David Easton's theoretical uses of the concept and conclude with comments on the work of Morton Kaplan and J. David Singer.

General Systems Theory originated as an attempt to find "the most general conceptual framework in which a scientific theory or a technological problem can be placed without losing the essential features of the theory or the problem."[1] This means in the first instance a search for analogies between models of the structure or behavior of physical systems, biological systems, or the relations in and between social and political groups. There is nothing remarkable in this as a program for action. Indeed, analogies have been useful tools in the process of science since its beginnings. Presumably they will continue to be used (and abused) whatever the ultimate fate of systems theory. The danger as always is that analogies may be used not just to suggest specific empirical hypotheses but to assert real isomorphic relations, i.e., that a one-to-one correspondence exists between the elements of two objects or relations and that the relations among the elements are preserved by this same correspondence. Thus we find one writer using the terms "entropy," "negative entropy" and "adaptation" as if the activities signified by these terms were formally identical with political behavior as applied to the study of regions.[2] Now this may very well turn out to be true but the contention cannot rest on mere assertion. On what then would it rest? The answer is that one would need to specify precisely the state of the particular system—in this case the relevant variables in the regional system—as well as precisely postulating the laws which govern the progression of the system. If an exact specification of the relations is known, it is then possible to portray the system as a particular mathematical model. Once this is done one could see at once whether the regional system in fact behaved like those physical models which do exhibit "entropy" or "adaptation."[3] Unless we can do something like the above we are left with an analogy or a series of them and nothing more.[4] It is tempting at this point to dismiss the whole general systems approach as a mere chimera or to demand that scholars pursuing this line of endeavor produce isomorphic relationships on pain of excommunication.[5] This would be a serious mistake. Our present state of knowledge permits precise specification of relevant variables in very few cases, formal theories of arms races being one notable exception.[6] To demand it is to demand the impossible and by so doing shut off potentially fruitful ideas. Arbitrary demands for rigor are simply not in order at this stage of the theoretical game. All that is necessary is for practitioners to stop talking about isomorphic relationships, accepting the fact that they are dealing with mere analogies, and proceed to suggest empirical connections among the relationships which they propose to study.

One of the most wide-ranging and sophisticated attempts to apply the concepts of modern systems theory to politics has been a number of studies by David Easton.[7] Easton sees his task as that of developing a unified theory of politics applicable to all political systems and particularly identifying the conditions for the survival of such systems. Political activity for Easton is a life process for which the perspectives of systems analysis serve to link all the sciences.[8] Like all living systems, the political system is seen as able to adjust to changes in its environment while retaining those characteristics which can identify it as the same system. Hence the approach is not a static equilibrium approach but is dynamic in nature.

For Easton, a political system is "a set of interactions abstracted from the totality of social behavior, through which values are allocated for a society"[9] and in which these value allocations are authoritative in the sense that subjects of the decision regard it as imperative to obey the decision.[10] The political system is seen as basically an input-output mechanism for such an allocation of values where inputs mean the demands made upon the system and outputs are the results of the processing of these demands. Hence to survive effectively a system must be able to deal with demand stress either in the form of information feedback from its own output or from the possible overload of input demands from the environment. It must also resist support stresses which come from failures of members, structural failures or failures to produce outputs in response to demands.[11] If stresses reach a "critical range" the allocation of values is disrupted to the point where "the society would collapse for want of a system of behavior to fulfill one of its vital functions."[12]

Obviously one of the key points for Easton's theory, if it is to be testable and therefore fruitful, is the concept of "critical range." For if this cannot be specified in operational terms there would be no way of knowing whether the system collapsed from a surfeit of demands, a failure in outputs, support stress or some combination of the three. Alas, on this crucial issue Easton retreats into ambiguity. For example, on the issue of minimal levels of support, he declares, in an incomprehensible and in the context contradictory phrase, that "even if adequacy of support is interpreted as an indeterminate but determinable minimal amount, it is not without its continued ambiguities."[13] This is described as a "recalcitrant" situation which defies analysis in black and white terms. It is not, it would appear, "a specific condition that occurs at a point in time or on a scale dividing viability from collapse" but as "a critical range within which a system or its objects may roam."[14] It may, he tells us, be better described "as a broad threshold, a limbo in which a system may linger. . . ." Despite these difficulties, the concept is, he maintains, empirically "plausible" even though it may only be possible to establish disappearance of minimal support "ex post facto."[15]

Now, amounts may be "indeterminate" but if they are described at the same time as "determinable," then one must be able to specify the conditions under which limits are to be defined. Hence the empirical problem cannot be dismissed by denying that adequacy of support is neither a "specific condition" nor a "scale" but "a critical range." "Specific conditions," if in fact they are made specific, can be described on "a scale" and, indeed, there can be no other meaning for a notion like "critical range" which implies a scalar measure, for without a scale we would not have a "range" at all but simply behavior occurring without measurement. In short, Easton's analysis fails at a critical point in terms of methodology. However interesting it may be, it remains a formal system, purely analytic and without the possibility of empirical contact with the real world unless its key concepts—such as "critical range"—can be given testable form.[16]

Finally, Easton postulates three structures of support in his system: the political community (a group of people who come together to solve the system's problems); the regime (the set of ideas or rules which forms a regular method of dealing with problems); the authorities (the group of individuals who assume responsibility for making decisions). The authorities process inputs and outputs with the help of subsystems such as private associations like trade unions and churches.

In the international system, Easton identifies the authorities as "the great powers and, more recently, various kinds of international organizations, such as the League of Nations and the United Nations [which] have been successful, intermittently, in resolving differences that were not privately negotiated and in having [their decisions] accepted as authoritative. It is they who have acted in the role of authorities."[17] He argues that the international system has a regime in that the relationships among the actors are "not random nor are their interactions without constraints." "Rules and expectations prevail, even though they may be less regularly complied with than in the many national systems."[18]

There is also an international political community which "possesses a theoretical status that is equivalent in every respect but one with the political systems of national societies." "It differs only in the fact that the component units of the international system consist of large and powerful subsystems that we call national political systems, and regional groupings of them."[19] For Easton the international system is "comparable in all respects to any other kind of system, *at the theoretical level*, although the values for the relevant variables will clearly be different."[20] Some disputes are resolved through the authoritative allocation of values; members put in demands and seek to have them converted into outputs, authorities are "less centralized," "less continuous in their operations" with the result that the international political system is akin to "primitive" political systems.[21]

There are some obvious difficulties in applying Easton's theory to the international system.[22] If we cannot identify the source of authoritative allocations for particular demands or if the authorities themselves are unstable, then the concept of system, *as postulated by Easton*, tends to disappear.[23] In international politics, key demands and key outputs are made and satisfied in the really critical cases by individually powerful members and these by Easton's own definition "would not have the compelling quality of authoritative allocations" and, therefore, their demands "would not be converted into recognized systemic outputs."[24] Possible exceptions to this criticism might be actions taken by the Security Council of the United Nations or, more importantly, the exercise of authority by the great powers at the end of major wars.[25] In such cases, since they possess overwhelming military power, they become for a short time the source of major decisions. They do allocate values but the imperative is military and not ethical and the guidelines are the balance of power. In the name of security they agree among themselves on the destruction or reconstruction of states, frontiers and governments, the transfer of populations, the new balance of military power and so on. This *is* a type of authority but it is not the sort envisaged by Easton. It is the authority of naked power, of force and the threat of force, an authority supported by fear and induced by exhaustion. It is, in fact, an authority which exists not as a right but as an enforced obedience. In between general wars that authority rests to a large extent upon the military dominance of the great powers, the influence which their superior power brings them, particularly their ability to maintain peace by a host of devices ranging from threats to intervention, the diplomacy of fear and favor and, sometimes, collusion among themselves for their larger strategic purposes. Thus a regime exists but except for the minimal constraints achieved by the rules of international law and diplomatic intercourse, the system obeys the rules of the balance of power to an overwhelming extent.

The end result is a system which processes many demands by force, which ignores stress until conflicting demands erupt into violent conflict or intense competition and in which outputs are often intermittent or, when they do occur, are based upon national perceptions and needs. In short, it is a system largely dominated by subsystems (states and their allies). Resource expenditures are concentrated at the top of the hierarchy of states and allocations are overwhelmingly military in nature with economic aid, propaganda, diplomacy and international institutions accounting for a tiny fraction of the total.[26] Feedback does exist but it is often negative in nature. For example, a "demand" in the shape of a 53-0 vote by the UN Conference on the Human Environment for a ten-year moratorium on the killing of whales and a "demand" in the form of a quota by the International Whaling Commission has been ignored by Japan and Russia, the two largest fishers of whales. The example is instructive and, alas, symptomatic of deep-seated patterns of behavior.

In sum, Easton's theoretical scheme does not correspond in significant ways with the realities of international life. Except in marginal ways, it fails to explain the data unless one is content with evidence which points in a negative direction.

Let us turn, therefore, to attempts which have been made to examine the international system from the standpoint of a system which operates according to balance-of-power principles. We have selected for examination the work of Morton A. Kaplan who has attempted with a certain degree of success to apply systems concepts to the phenomena.[27]

Kaplan's work attempts to avoid the almost insuperable difficulties of general theory by developing comparative theories of different systems. As one early reviewer (an economist by training) noted, Kaplan "tries to treat international politics piecemeal by partial-equilibrium methods."[28] The models, however, are *not* static equilibrium models but rather are designed to respond to change "within specified limits, by maintaining or restoring system equilibrium."[29] In form the models are deductive in that abstract propositions are enunciated which specify relationships among variables in different types of international systems.[30] The models are hypothetical only, i.e., they are abstract, analytical tools and, therefore, must be capable of being adopted or interpreted to the empirical world if they are to be of much theoretical use.[31]

Kaplan's models present six different types of international systems—the balance of power system, the loose bipolar system, the tight bipolar system, the universal system, the hierarchical system, and the unit veto system. The models use five sets of variables—the essential rules (which state the behavior necessary to maintain equilibrium in the system); the transformation rules (which state the changes which occur in the system as inputs and which move the system toward instability or toward a new system); the actor classificatory variables (which specify the structural characteristics of the actors, e.g., nation-state, alliance, etc.); finally, variables which specify the capabilities of the actors and available information.

It is essential, in order to understand fully what Kaplan is trying to do, to grasp the fact that there are three kinds of equilibrium in such systems: (1) equilibrium within the set of essential rules so that if behavior occurs which breaks the rule then one or more of the essential rules will be changed; (2) equilibrium in the sense that, although a change in the set of rules occurs, this will produce a change in other characteristics of the system and vice versa; (3) equilibrium in the sense that the system is in equilibrium with its environment so that changes in the system will change the environment and vice versa.

It is obvious that such a wide use of "equilibrium" has its dangers. It leads to confusion in particular instances as to which of the three meanings is involved and a good deal of the criticism of Kaplan's work can be traced to this source. A more serious difficulty, however, is raised by asking whether the three definitions taken together produce a series of tautologies in the precise sense that it is difficult to conceive of what objections could be raised which would refute assertions that this or that aspect of the model is in fact in equilibrium. That is to say, the wide use of the term equilibrium presents a standing temptation to preserve the models from refutation by passing back and forth between the three meanings as the situation demands. Models which do not present clear ways of differentiating between the equilibrium of rules, system characteristics and environment will resist empirical tests. This will be true even if we realize, as Kaplan clearly does, that the theories can be used to derive consequences only if the boundary conditions are explicitly stated. In sum, severe difficulties have been placed in the path of empirical tests by the manner in which the models have been defined.

With this caveat firmly in mind, let us now examine one of Kaplan's models—the balance of power. It has six characteristics: the actors are nation states; the goals are oriented toward the optimization of security in the sense of a preference for survival; weapons are conventional; unpredictable increases in productivity occur; there must be at least five major nations in order to keep war limited; each state requires allies. These characteristics give rise, Kaplan believes, to six essential rules:

(1) Act to increase capabilities but negotiate rather than fight.

(2) Fight rather than pass up an opportunity to increase capabilities.

(3) Stop fighting rather than eliminate an essential national actor.

(4) Act to oppose any coalition or essential actor that tends to assume a position of predominance with respect to the system.

(5) Act to constrain actors who subscribe to supranational organizing principles.

(6) Permit defeated or constrained essential national actors to re-enter the system as acceptable role partners or act to bring some previously inessential actor within the essential actor classification. Treat all essential actors as acceptable role partners.[32]

Before going farther in the analysis, let us subject these rules to cursory examination. Of course, from one point of view Kaplan can enunciate any rules he likes and, if they do the theoretical work intended, the selection should be accepted as it stands. But, assuming difficulties ahead, some insights into the adequacy of the model can be gained if we ask the following questions of the list: Do the rules contradict one another? Are any of them unnecessary in a logical sense? And, finally, could we suggest any substitute rules which might improve the model?

One early critic suggested that there is an obvious contradiction between Rules (1) and (2)[33] and suggested that Rule (2) should read "Fight rather than submit to a substantial loss in capabilities." If Kaplan has accepted this criticism, it has escaped our notice but it is an incisive suggestion since it removes a clear contradiction and moves closer to what states seem to do in actuality. The original rule (2) is "neither rational or reasonable" as Aron points out.[34]

There seems also to be a potential ambiguity when one considers Rules (3) and (6) together. That is, an actor would not know *from the rules alone as stated* whether to stop fighting rather than eliminate a rival or to go ahead and then bring in a previously inessential great power. To repeat, this is not a contradiction as such on one reading of the rules but rather is a case where the rules themselves are ambiguous in the sense of not dictating a clear course of action. In practice states did hesitate to eliminate a rival great power but "inessential" actors often entered as the result of a general war into which they were drawn willy-nilly. Certainly actors often clearly preferred to increase capabilities rather than fight (thus contradicting Rule (2)) as when Britain signed the Anglo-Japanese alliance in order to concentrate the fleet more effectively in home waters.

One critic has indicated a desire to eliminate Rule (3) on the ground that it simply expresses the principle of equilibrium.[35] This seems much too facile a criticism as it stands. The proper question is rather this: What exactly is meant by the words which indicate that an actor should oppose the attempt "to assume a position of predominance with respect to the rest of the system?" What precisely does the notion entail? One of the most learned scholars of the balance of power, the late Martin Wight, put the matter thus: "There should be no crippling superiorities of power among the members of the state system,"[36] with this to mean such an increase that a majority, if not a single state, could not coerce any member. To judge the limits of change was "the highest art of the statesman."[37] Thus Wight's language reveals clearly as Kaplan's does not that Rule (4) as it stands is obscure and conceals the fact that a major clue to the operation of the system lies in the relative changes in the power of the actors. Large increases of power will threaten the system's stability. If no specific ways exist to test the degrees of growth or superiority which will be tolerated, then we are thrown back on the subjective judgment indicated by Wight and Kaplan's model becomes untestable. Therefore, unless we can develop a rule of toleration, that captures the extent to which a resource increase will be permitted and its proportions relative to the capabilities of member states, we will be left with a purely formal model. The key nature of capability increases is further demonstrated by the fact that Rule (5) (constraint of states which espouse "supranational" [revolutionary?] principles) is ignored in fact when it conflicts with Rule (6) (treat all as acceptable allies) as in 1939 when Nazi Germany and the Soviet Union signed a form of alliance.

It seems highly doubtful, therefore, whether the rules as stated can account for the behavior of states in the balance of power. In his later work Kaplan attempts to explain discrepancies by what he calls "engineering the model."[38] By this he means changing the parameters to account for deviations observed in the real world. For example, he accounts for the failure of Germany and France to consider one another as potential allies after 1870 as due to the use of revanchist opinion over Alsace-Lorraine and, indeed, as the reason why war aims became unlimited. Whether this is the kind of adaptation permitted is questionable. Taken together with the objections raised above, it suggests to these authors the need for a new model rather than a mere adjustment in the existing theory.

The remainder of Kaplan's approach is less attractive, being filled with jargon and relatively innocuous hypotheses. National actors are described as "directive" (read "dictatorial") and "non-directive" (read democratic). The form tends to be hierarchical with directives (i.e., orders) flowing downwards. Systems have two sub-categories: system dominant (meaning that it is dominant over its subsystems, in the sense that its rules must be accepted) and subsystem dominant (where the parties need not obey the rules). Thus the United States is a non-directive, system dominant national actor in Kaplan's terms relative to NATO.

Clearly these categories are much too broad as they stand. The United States, for example, was "directive" over withdrawal of Anglo-French forces from Egypt in 1956. It is generally "non-directive" over NATO and it certainly has not been "system dominant" over issues like troop levels in the latter organization.

Similar difficulties arise with Kaplan's attempt to classify international actions in six classes which are then related to the types of actors and the different types of systems. These classes are: the organizational focus of decisions (available resources, objects and instruments of policy; the way rewards are allocated; preferences for cooperation; level of activity (active or indifferent states); adaptive and non-adaptive behavior.

Applied to the balance of power system, Kaplan predicts that "the directive, subsystem dominant actor will extend its primary attention to external considerations" whereas "the non-directive, system dominant actor will pay primary attention to internal considerations in the formulation of policy."[39] Is it really so obvious that significant differences exist between the super-powers with respect to the primacy of foreign policy considerations? Soviet policy seems to be oriented heavily toward internal requirements at the time of writing as indicated by the wheat deal whereas for a long period in 1968–72 American policy in Vietnam seems to have ignored internal considerations in the carrying out of policy decided (however mistakenly) on strategic grounds.

In the realm of allocation, Kaplan argues that "directive subsystem dominant actors" (for example, the Soviet Union) will identify bloc and national interests and will "tend to subordinate [national] interests to those of the bloc less than does the non-directive national actor."[40] This seems to mean that dominant actors can do pretty much what they like with their satellites (which is hardly news) but it would be interesting to try and list those cases in which the United States subordinated its interests to those of its allies. A comparison might show relatively small differences between the super-powers in most cases.

In considering the processes of systems, Kaplan describes a "regulatory" process "by means of which a system attempts to maintain or preserve its identity over time as it adapts to changing conditions."[41] This capacity measures the range of responses available in meeting disturbances to the system's equilibrium. This capacity relates to the way in which structural elements are arranged. Kaplan finds that "directive systems" will "consider and adjust to more external factors than the non-directive system."[42] The reason, according to Kaplan, is that directive systems have a better division of labor in the sense that each decision-maker pays closer attention to the specialized aspects of problems. How Kaplan knows whether Soviet leaders pay closer attention to specialized aspects of problems than their American counterparts is something of a mystery or how, indeed, one could go about ascertaining the truth of this statement. On the surface it seems a highly dubious assertion. Further, one would think that American policy has considered and adjusted to a much larger range of external facts than the Soviet Union—at least until very recently. It has had greater resources, world-wide military capabilities and, of course, a much larger network of alliances and client states. At this point then, Kaplan's theory seems inadequate and clearly led astray by mistaken assumptions.

Systems, according to Kaplan, are subject to integrative and disintegrative processes, these being defined as processes which provide for the common pursuit of some goals or policies or which fail to do so. The existence of either depends on whether there are common interests or not and the degree and extent of communications between members. Integration and stability go together with the latter occurring when the system satisfies the values of members and of the whole system. A list of nine hypotheses is then suggested. These are uniformly uninteresting, such as the idea that people who occupy a number of roles see matters in a more connected manner than do persons who occupy a single role or that conflict is greater the less the integration within and between systems.[43] These are then applied to the balance of power system and reveal that actual or impending conflict characterizes that system. Integration is performed by the balancer who prevents preponderance by swapping alliance partners. Solidarity and integration processes are minimized by the small number of actors because one wrong decision can have momentous results. Larger numbers would reduce disintegrative effects. Decrease in numbers leads to deceit, suspicion, intrigue and inconsistent patterns of action.

All this leads to the question "How does one know when one system becomes another system?" Kaplan claims that his theory provides transformation rules which suggest how each model could be changed into "worlds analyzable by each of the other models."[44] This seems much too sweeping a claim. Moreover, the claim is in fact hedged by Kaplan himself since he says that his work "leaves open whether the phases of the real world to which the different models are applied should be considered real system changes or merely different equilibrium states of one ultra-stable international system."[45] The key question, therefore, becomes "Is the change reversible?" If so, it is an equilibrium change. If not, then it is a change of system. Kaplan sees this issue clearly but seems unwilling to admit that a set of transformation rules which leave the issue of reversibility in doubt is inadequate.

Finally, let us consider more of the work which J. David Singer has done in the area of systems analysis.[46] His work is marked by clarity and rigor in understanding the nature of theory and by a shrewd appraisal of the limits of our present knowledge. For example, Singer insists that analysis should focus on *events* and *entities* as distinct from actions, behavior, roles, decision-making, etc. To try the latter approach is to run into serious procedural problems for one has to identify and specify those persons who interact, behave and so on before one can describe the phenomena. One also has to differentiate between various systems, subsystems and classes of action before analysis can begin. The result is to move back and forth between different types often without clear criteria in mind with the result that confusion reigns supreme. This difficulty is then compounded by the fact that systems analysis based on activities usually involves categories which unwittingly include several levels of analysis which should be distinct but usually are not.[47]

Singer is keenly aware that general systems theory often assumes too great similarities between systems or becomes so abstract as to be virtually meaningless. These facts, combined with the previous difficulties outlined for the action approach to systems, lead him to begin with partial theories which study behavioral events or act as interaction sequences. This means, among other things, that Singer sees the first task of a systems analysis as that of accurate description which he believes must precede efforts at explanation.[48]

Thus, when Singer tackles the problem of war he begins by defining the social system as "any aggregation of individuals or groups who manifest a modest degree of interdependence, similarity, or common destiny, and whose treatment as a single unit is scientifically useful to the researcher."[49] He postulates a *global* system (all of mankind and any of the worldwide groups which men have formed), the *international* system (all national political units; all of the people in these nations, and any sub-national and extra-national groups of interest), the *interstate* system (all those natural entities that satisfy certain criteria of statehood as well as the individuals, sub-national and extra-national groups within these states). Within the interstate system are two subsystems—the central system and the major power system.

Singer then goes on to specify exact criteria for deciding on membership in these various systems as well as a typology of war which discriminates between interstate, central system and imperial and colonial wars. Thus by these rigorous methods Singer is able to specify in clear, operational terms the phenomena he is attempting to describe—whether a political entity is a member of the inter-state system, its degree of participation, the different types of war in which it engaged and so on. The end result is a prime example of fundamental research which provides an accurate data base on which theories on the causes of war can be advanced and, hopefully, subjected to empirical test. The next step, therefore, will be to discover which variables or clusters of variables show the strongest and most consistent association with fluctuations in the incidence of war over the century and a half under study.[50] Once these patterns are ascertained it may be possible to differentiate between events and conditions which led to war and those which did not.

In this search Singer will utilize four basic sets of data: (1) the physical, structural and cultural attributes of the international system, which will describe the state of the latter and its direction and rate of change; (2) the attributes or characteristics of nations, which may indicate types that are more war-prone than others; (3) the fluctuating relationships between specific pairs and clusters of nations, which will reflect types of interdependence and (4) the behavioral and interaction sequences which characterize conflict processes which may identify those modes of behavior which more regularly lead to war or to peace.[51]

The program of research outlined is immensely difficult and time-consuming. It may well prove to be an insuperable task. But the approach used, which applies systems concepts to discrete phenomena and in the end provides us with partial theories of how the international system actually operates, may prove to be the only feasible way of developing a general theory of international politics.

7
The International Impact of American Theory

The international system[1] consists of approximately 150 nation-states; one inter-governmental organization (the United Nations) made up at present of 149 of the nation-states; 6 or more regional organizations of nation-states; a large number of non-governmental organizations such as the International Red Cross and the International Chamber of Commerce; and, finally, another large number of multinational corporations. These components of the international system are commonly called its subsystems, and each subsystem may have sub-systems.

This breakdown is unavoidably imprecise because the numerical composition of each subsystem varies significantly over time.

The system and all its subsystems are designed to meet needs perceived by the human individuals or groups (the so-called "elites") who make decisions for the system or subsystem. The nation-state has much the longest history of all the categories and commands the greatest devotion of its members. It is in consequence also the most peremptory in the definition and pursuit of what its decision-makers call "national interests." Their claims in the name of the state to prestige, *Lebensraum* and access to materials and markets have made violence an endemic feature of the international system. Finding temporary and partial communities of interest, nation-states have from time immemorial formed limited and fluctuating alliances for security or aggression. A frequent object of such alliances is to "balance" the power of a state or combination of states that is becoming threateningly strong. This is the familiar see-saw of the "balance of power."

Despite many famous paper plans of permanent organization to control the international use of force, it was not until 1918 that such organization became official policy. Even then national governments were unwilling to accept the limitations upon state sovereignty and to endow the "collective-security" organization with the authority and material power that could alone give prospect of success. The League of Nations crashed in a second world war. Its successor, the United Nations, despite a Charter that promised to correct major weaknesses of the League, has in its thirty-one years of operation increasingly displayed a tendency to surrender first to the arrogant sovereignty of its strongest members and then to an organized majority of weak states seeking their particular ends. While the need for supranational control has been multiplied by the development of nuclear weapons, the accelerated pollution of the biosphere, and the exhaustion of material resources, the organization designed to secure peace and welfare for a world community is sabotaged by the arrogant postures of a type of national political organization which daily demonstrates its obsolescence as the chief instrumentality of human security and welfare.

The political development that in the long process of time produced the nation-state had its beginnings in that remote period when *homo sapiens* was evolving in small groups separated by geographical features that prevented intercommunication and led to the formation of different languages and to different modes of adaptation to varying environments. As such groups became aware of one another, the stranger was an enemy and warfare was the normal relation. Special skills enabled some groups to dominate others, and in time empires were formed spreading one language and one culture over wide areas. But always dominance brought with it luxury, internal conflict, and eventually laxity: empires fell apart, reassembled under different leadership and fell apart again. Destruction followed creation. None of the accompanying slaughter and devastation has yet taught mankind that it must unite under universal political authority and power or perish. Men still cling to traditions and cultures that are grotesquely unsuited to the conditions of our time.

For the last half-century legal, social and political theorists have been increasingly busy trying to identify the determinants of political behavior and to prescribe norms and structures for its control. Their efforts, though widely differing in method and focus, have thrown new light upon the nature and multiplicity of these determinants. Elaborate formulas of cause and effect have been worked out with the aim of enabling decision-making elites to predict and prepare for situations with which they will be called upon to deal. The common object, sought along contending approaches, is to replace the erring traditional, intuitive formation of policy with impersonal equations approaching mathematical precision. Indeed the apex of the thrust is such a quantification of all the factors entering into decision-making as will make the computer the essential instrument for action.

This is not to say that any generally accepted theory of world politics has been achieved. In the United States, where the contemporary movement has been most active, the debate about the identification and weighting of dependent and independent variables, parameters, feedbacks positive and negative, etc., becomes at times elegantly vituperative.[2] Despite some official experiments with games theory and simulation models, there is little evidence that the new thought has significantly changed the traditional processes of policy-making.

Meanwhile, students entering the field of international studies are inclined to skimp what has traditionally been regarded as a necessary preparation in the history and legal systems of our vast ancestry of political societies. The earliest possible elevation to high theory becomes the common ambition. Their mentors, often themselves distinguished scholars, do not always exact an adequate preliminary equipment. They are also rather apt to undervalue approaches other than their own. If there is one position which they appear to share it is a somewhat contemptuous rejection of the world federalist movement. Even if an effective system of world government were feasible, which they deny, it would, they argue, necessarily mean dictatorial control by a succession of dominant powers. In practice, the result would be little improvement, if any, over the present international system.

Admitting all the difficulties of subordinating the state to supranational control, and the possibility of abusive appropriation of such control, there is still much to be said for the world-federalists. They are doing at least as much as any other movement to educate people in the need for political machinery capable, as the congeries of sovereign states is not, of meeting the desperately urgent problems of human survival and welfare. Their direct appeal to revolutionary, though peaceful, change may well have more practical effect on the behavior of governments than the formulas of the high theorists. In any event there is no good reason why the various approaches should not be employed simultaneously and with mutual respect.

Since the avowed object of each of the contending American schools of thought on the international system is a universally acceptable theory of all or part of its operation, we might have expected a serious effort to communicate with European and other specialists in the field. In fact, there has been a tendency in the United States to assume that progressive foreign thought in the social sciences came to an end with such masters as Weber and his contemporaries, and that any hope of future advance rests with American thinkers, many of whom are of course recent imports. This absence of inter-change has been noted by European writers with critical explanations that will be referred to later. The authors of this book are convinced that continuous and friendly dialogue with social scientists in other countries would not merely qualitatively strengthen the American contribution, but is an essential condition of progress towards a rationally structured and directed world community. It is with the hope of stimulating such interchange that we now present some assessments of recent American thought by foreign scholars who have attempted to interpret it for their colleagues.

In an address at the University of Padua in 1962 Professor B. H. M. Vlekke of Leyden, after remarking that modern theories of international relations were being elaborated for the most part in the United States, proceeded to a drastically negative evaluation. No theory of social science, he insisted, could ever have the precision of the exact sciences or escape a necessarily speculative character. The great defect of such theorists as Morton Kaplan, Thomas Schelling, Richard Snyder and Stanley Hoffman was hasty generaliza-tion. He was suspicious of all policy-oriented research and all concep-tions of political science as a means of predicting the future and serving governments in the solution of political problems. The object of political study should be to train, not ministers of government, but intelligent citizens.

The dismissal of policy-oriented research is of course a reference to Professor Myers McDougal and his Yale school. It so happens that the work of that group has attracted marked attention and increasingly analytical study in the European literature of law and political science. The progression from puzzled interest to competent critique may be traced from Manuel Medina Ortega in *Revista Española de Derecho Internacional*, 14 (1961), pp. 517–33, and 36 *Revista Juridica de la Universidad de Puerto Rico* (1967), pp. 1–39, to Bent Rosenthal's *Etude de "Oeuvre de Myers Smith McDougal en Matière de Droit International Public* (Paris, 1970).

Medina hails McDougal's sociological approach as the embodiment of a new conception of international law and the most important contemporary American contribution to the subject. He compares it to George Scelle's derivation of legal rules from the social fact—that union of ethics and power (social solidarity) without which no positive law can exist. McDougal's constant emphasis upon values may, he thinks, find special welcome among Spanish scholars because of their traditional respect for natural law. A warning, however, is necessary. McDougal's public order of human dignity is no abstract model. It is a concrete, operating order in a society characterized by general participation in political power. Moreover, Medina finds some partisanship in the Yale school due to what he considers an inevitable special interest in the positions taken by the United States in world politics. What he counsels, therefore, is neither enthusiastic reception nor total rejection, but a detached interest in what may prove the best way to a value-oriented reconstruction of the international order.

Much the most searching examination and evaluation of the work of McDougal and his colleagues is that of the Danish diplomat and scholar, Bent Rosenthal. This book, written in the language that still vies with English as the common tongue of diplomacy and presented, before publication in Paris, as a doctoral thesis in the Faculty of Law there, is an heroic effort to interpret to the civil-law world what the author considers a new and vitally important statement of the nature and operation of law in the international power process.[3]

Rosenthal reserves his highest praise for the realism and exactitude of McDougal's description of the way in which legal decisions are made in the international arena. He is sceptical about the fusion of law and policy, holding, as some American critics have, that this lends a fluidity to law that defeats its ordering purpose. In the constant insistence upon values he finds a natural-law influence, but observes the formal emptiness of the value-criterion in a doctrine that allows the decision-maker a latitude practically unfettered by pre-established rules—limited in fact only by the vague and shifting standard of reasonableness—in assessing, adjusting or adjudicating opposing claims. Even the expectations founded upon previous approved practice—expectations in which McDougal finds a principal source of authority—may be defeated by the unavoidable subjectivity of this process. Rosenthal indeed discovers in the leader of the Yale school an intense nationalism, asserting that most of the positions he assumes on actual international problems are designed to justify American policy. Here, however, Rosenthal displays a balance not to be found in the review by Meyrowitz, much less in the Russian studies that we shall presently examine. Thus, while he finds McDougal asserting the legality of the action taken by the United States in the Security Council's 1950 Resolution on Korea, in the Southeast Asia interventions, in the "quarantine" of Cuba and in the non-recognition of the Chinese People's Republic, he also records his criticism of the atomic attack upon Hiroshima, and of the negative American stance on the genocide and human rights conventions.

We turn now to a German critique. This is by Knud Krakau, Referent in the Institute of Foreign Politics, Hamburg, whose book, *Missionsbewusstsein und Völkerrechtsdoktrin in den Vereinigten Staaten von Amerika*, was published (Frankfort, Berlin) in 1967.

Citing Chinese, Hindu and Buddhist indifference to improvement,

Krakau rejects the assumption of a universal human will to maximize values. This *a priori* starting-point is a product peculiar to Christian-Western culture generally and to the American-Puritan credo of progress in particular. McDougal is activated by a characteristically American sense of mission. His functional approach, to be sure, is a great step towards escape from the sterile conceptualism of traditional legal theory, but his negation of any binding quality in established norms and the reduction of law to a succession of *ad hoc* decisions subject the whole decision-making process to the particular ideology of the decision-maker. This means no common law but an arbitrary subjectivity usually justifying national policy. What then becomes of that minimum world order of human dignity that is McDougal's declared objective?

AMERICAN POLITICAL SCIENCE AND SOVIET POLITICAL THOUGHT

At the University of Leningrad in September 1946, one of the present writers asked a professor of political economy whether he taught political theory and, if so, what theories he surveyed. The Russian, a quiet man in his forties, only three months back from active military service, was startled. Rising quickly from his chair, he swung an arm around the huge portraits of Marx, Engels and Lenin adorning his office and said, "Those are my political theory."

In the Soviet Union political economy is economics and, though no student could escape a drilling in Marx-Leninism, no such title as *Politicheskaya Nauka* (political science) appeared in the curriculum. There is not yet, so far as we are aware, any official recognition of such a discipline, though there has been a serious academic move in that direction.

In 1965, Professor F. M. Burlatski published in *Pravda* (January 10) an article urging the systematic study and analysis of the state and society, covering all the main factors determining the formation and execution of domestic and foreign policy in capitalist as well as communist countries. This was a plea for the recognition and active pursuit of a science of politics, though the author emphasized that his purpose was not so much the recognition of an independent discipline as "the profound study and analysis of the problems that constitute the field of political science."

In 1970 the same author brought out, under the auspices of the Academy of Sciences, a book on which he asserts he had spent more than ten years of work and which, despite its disarmingly narrow title, *Lenin, Gosudarstvo, Politica* (*Lenin, State, Politics*) presents in its more than five hundred pages a distinguished example of the kind of study he had advocated in the article of 1965.[4]

This scholarly work makes it abundantly clear that Soviet specialists in the social sciences have kept a sharp eye on German, French, English and American political writing of the last forty years. Summing up this bourgeois literature, Burlatski concedes that the new sociological analysis of what is actually being done in the name of the state is an important step forward from the traditional study of formal rules and structures. This restrained tribute is immediately qualified by what has become a tiresomely familiar refrain. The essential purpose of the change is to bolster the defences of the existing capitalist order. Yet, despite his due and repeated animadversions on the capitalist-monopoly state and its dedicated apologists, Burlatski is holding up the political science of the Western world as an example of the wide-ranging research and interpretation that he urges upon his Soviet colleagues. His book is a protest against a system of political education that merely expounds received gospel.

Among American writers Burlatski cites Merriam, Lasswell, Friedrich, Lippman, Loewenstein, Sydney Hook, Lip From, Riesman, Snyder, Brzezinski, Lipset, Huntington and Simon. Strangely enough, he has nothing to say about McDougal and the Yale school, though he does mention, in his extensive bibliography, O. R. Young's *Systems of Political Science*. The book ends with twenty-four pages of bibliography, the last seven being devoted to Western publications, many of which had escaped notice in the text.

Much more outspoken in its condemnation is V. Kalenski's *Politicheskaya Nauka v S Sh A*, Moscow, 1969. The purpose of this 103-page tract is clearly stated on the flyleaf and repeated at intervals throughout the text. It is to demonstrate how the bourgeois political scientists of the United States are more and more making it their task to provide new intellectual weapons for the imperialists in their struggle to maintain control of the masses.

Like Burlatski, Kalenski finds American political science grossly defective in its failure to recognize the essentially class nature of bourgeois government. But this is more than a scientific fault. The picture of contemporary capitalist-monopoly government as expressing the will of the whole society rather than a ruling clique is a conscious attempt to justify and stiffen governmental resistance to worker-demand. Easton, Dahl, Schattschneider, Almond, Verba, W. Rostow and Parsons are all tainted with subjective prejudice as well as scientific error.

The communist attack upon the Yale school, fittingly enough in view of that group's concentration upon international law and relations, was reserved for the Soviet Union's best known international lawyer. In his monograph, *Ideologicheskaya Borba i Mezhdunarodnogo Pravo*, 1967, and again in *Teoriya Mezhdunarodnoga Prava* (1970 edition), G. I. Tunkin applies to the work of Professor McDougal and his associates all the strictures aimed by Burlatski and Kalenski at American political science in general. There is indeed a degree of similarity that indicates concerted and officially approved strategy. Bourgeois legal science refuses to recognize the class nature of law and thus fails to reveal its true social character. This is indeed a willed failure, for to reveal the class nature of bourgeois law would be to oppose it. McDougal's fusion of law and policy is unscientific. It is designed to justify, in terms of international law, any sort of violation of that order. As examples of such justification he cites the defense of interventions in Vietnam and the Dominican Republic. Turning to Richard Falk's *Legal Order in a Violent World*, he finds the author in general agreement with McDougal's approach, but notes with some approval his frequent disagreement on points of specific application especially on the role of the national elite in the interpretation of international law.

In view of his sharp attack on McDougal's doctrine as one designed and used to justify American violations of the international legal order, it is intriguing to read in this same volume (p. 498) Tunkin's defense of the Brezhnev doctrine covering the 1968 intervention in Czechoslovakia. The sovereignty of the socialist states, he argues in a *tour de force* of casuistry, is a sort of corporate quality peculiar to their community. One would look far for a more complete fusion of law and policy or a better example of the clash of theory and reality. Moscow marches in and forces a reversal of Czech policy, but commits no infringement of sovereignty or independence.[5]

Yet with all their ideological bluster, these Soviet writers manifest an underlying understanding of the recent American work on politics and law. There is in their description and evaluation more than a suggestion of carefully controlled desire for similar liberty of research and criticism.[6] As we have seen, they are far from alone in their scientific objection to the treatment of law as a policy science or in their rejection of the findings of legality in the initiation and conduct of American interventions in Indochina and elsewhere. Many American jurists join them in the substance of their criticism without following them into the absurd ritualistic accusations of uniform and complete dedication to the defense of imperialist, monopoly capitalist-government.

We have selected for comment three of the most distinguished contemporary Russian theorists. The study of American political science by no means ends with them. One excellent place in which to follow it is in the periodical *Sovietskoe Gosudarstvo i Pravo* with its eight or ten numbers a year. Thus the anonymous author of "Pravo b Ideologicheskoi Borbe Sovremennosti" in No. 10 of 1971, pp. 10–19, adds to Burlatski's plea a special exhortation to Soviet jurists and political scientists to watch the efforts of their bourgeois counterparts to defend their principles and forms of government. He selects for particular attack what he calls the bourgeois thesis of the incompatibility of socialist government and law and the doctrine of convergence between socialist and capitalist systems. D. A. Kerimov and H. M. Keiserov join in a similar onslaught in No. 1 of 1972, pp. 20–29, under the uncompromising title of "Nestoyatelnost Burzhuaznich Konseptsii Demokratii" ["The Invalidity of the Bourgeois Conceptions of Democracy"], while in No. 4 of the same year S. B. Marinin gives a realistic analysis of "The Bureaucratization of the Executive Apparatus in the United States."

Obviously our experience as well as our writing continues to excite a watchful interest among the "politologs" of the USSR.

The list of books and articles could be extended indefinitely, but we conclude with V. G. Graphskii's contribution to *Sovietskoe Gosudarstvo i Pravo*, No. 4, 1974, pp. 121–6. This is a virulent attack upon the doctrine of convergence, particularly as formulated by Z. Brzezinski and his colleagues, where it is essentially identical with monopoly-capitalist absorption of the socialist system. The author grudgingly admits some modification of Brzezinski's earlier doctrine in that he no longer holds the Soviet Fascist and Nazi dictatorships quite identical in their effects, though he still finds more similarities than differences between them. But he ridicules the thought that Soviet evolution towards a less totalitarian and dictatorial system could be hastened if the Western world, and especially the United States, adopted a policy of peaceful penetration and "bridge building." This he characterizes as a desperate effort to preserve a doomed system. Finally, citing articles in *Foreign Affairs* for October 1973, he finds Brzezinski and his fellow kremlinologists guilty of cold-war-mongering and advocating the continued growth of American military superiority. In comparison with his diatribe, the earlier Russian studies of political thought in the United States are moderation itself. Has the Kremlin dictated a harsher tone?[7]

8
Force, Strategy and Politics

In the year 1975 the world spent 345 billion dollars on military security, an amount which exceeded the totals spent on public education or health care.[1] Considered in itself, it is a staggering reflection on the priorities of mankind. When considered in the context of history, it becomes profoundly disturbing because these figures reflect a long-term trend toward the militarization of the state system. In .the past century there has occurred a doubling in the share of resources devoted to military purposes as opposed to other expenditures and there are few signs that the end is in sight.[2]

These brute facts reflect the preoccupation of states and particularly the great powers with the role of military power in either protecting themselves from coercion or in attempting to coerce others. This preoccupation with the uses of force has led to a vast outpouring of books and articles on strategic questions ranging from the specialized writings of professional military officers to commentaries upon the widest reaches of public policy.[3]

One commentator, oppressed by the constant discussion of strategic issues, remarks: "There exists in Washington a superficial glibness about strategy. Almost everyone is a military strategist. It has been taken up socially like the wig. Congressmen who hardly have the wit to tie their shoestrings rattle off such words as 'deterrent,' 'first strike,' 'counter force.' The barber or the taxi-driver knows exactly how to check the Russians. Professors lecture on pre-emptive wars to women's clubs."[4] In short, just as everyman is his own historian or theologian, everyman has become his own strategist.

It seems necessary, therefore, to issue a few words of warning to the unwary reader. Much of the best writing on strategic issues is highly abstract. It often ignores or is neutral about moral issues as well as the political setting in which action is considered or proposed. Much of it is "foreign to the world of political judgments. . . . There is little place in it for such considerations as the psychology of decision-making in crises, the persistence of traditional measures of strength, the role of intangibles like prestige and political momentum. Yet these are the stuff of political judgments."[5] This means among other things that to be useful strategic thinking must be evaluated within a political context if serious errors are to be avoided. An analysis which is confined to purely military matters is likely to leave out critical factors and hence produce fallacious results.[6]

Perhaps as important are the methods by which conclusions are reached in most strategic analysis. Much of it deals with nuclear war or its possibility. No large-scale nuclear war having occurred, no body of data on real events exists on which to base a common-sense analysis.[7] This means that analysts are forced to use simplified models to represent the real world and there is no way of knowing whether the models are sufficiently close to the real world to enable accurate conclusions to be reached. All the conclusions, therefore, should be looked at with considerable skepticism since their validity cannot be clearly established. Much of their analysis is simply personal intuition dressed up in pseudo-scientific garb.[8] We can be neither certain nor sure concerning either their conclusions or their recommendations.[9] Realization of this fact is the beginning of wisdom in any study of these grave matters.

It is not an accident that some of the clearest and most acute analyses of the changing role of force have been produced by students with an historical background.[10] This is so because some of the forces and trends responsible for changed conditions can be clearly observed over several decades and because the full implications of new technical developments are only gradually understood by those who make authoritative decisions.

For example, technology before 1914 had begun to introduce rapid changes in military hardware, made planning increasingly complex, placed a high premium on ready forces and enormous emphasis on untested weapons which were thought to be decisive in some aspects of war (the Dreadnought).[11]

The 1914–18 war disabused the thinking of those who believed conflicts would be short and decisive. Total war ending only through the given process of attrition became the central concept in men's minds. Airpower and attacks on civilians gave a foretaste of the future, and the conflict became virtually global in its extent.

The enormous costs of the first world war both in terms of

human lives and resources produced a widespread aversion to the use of war as an instrument of national policy. In practical political terms, British and French statesmen were reluctant to use mass war for anything but the objective of national survival. Hence, a statesman like Hitler, whose aversion to the use of force was imperceptible, could and did exploit the threat of war to achieve limited gains.[12] In the end, of course, he was compelled to face a conflict more terrible and more destructive than that of 1914.

It seems reasonable to argue, therefore, that the present "reluctance to contemplate the use of [nuclear weapons] is a continuation, although vastly intensified, of the reluctance to use the older techniques of mass war."[13] It does not, however, follow that nuclear weapons will not be any more effective as a deterrent to disturbances of the international order than was mass war in the 1930s.[14] Differences between the two types of war—conventional and nuclear—are so enormous as to be differences in kind. In 1939 a significant lead in men and weapons could be exploited both militarily and diplomatically. Victory was still a possible goal and total destruction of a society was only a remote possibility, not the logical concomitant of existing means. Present weapons are global in range and capable of destroying entire societies within the space of hours or even minutes. Their combination of speed and vast destruction makes an effective defense of populated areas almost impossible in the sense that such defenses would have to be nearly 100 per cent effective and could be counteracted either through saturation or through the use of penetration devices.[15] The end result is a conclusion which admits of little argument: full-scale nuclear war is not a rational policy choice.[16] This amounts to saying that nuclear weapons must be regarded as having only a deterrent function.

The concept of deterrence is as old as war itself and its central idea is simple enough: deterrence operates if the perceived and probable cost of achieving an objective outweighs the perceived and possible value of the objective. Pre-nuclear ideas of deterrence rested on war-making capability and since costs, though high, were often judged not prohibitive, effective deterrence usually rested on judgments concerning the probability of success. With nuclear weapons the terms of the calculation have changed since the probability of disastrous effects upon the group attacked is no longer debatable, and because of the high probability that the attacker would be attacked in turn with disastrous results.[17]

This is now taken for granted but the basic logic of nuclear deterrence was only developed after a long period of analysis, and the actual implementation of policy decisions on the structure and use of armed forces often lagged well behind the arguments of theorists. Thus, Bernard Brodie realized very early that, whereas the chief purpose of pre-nuclear forces had been to win wars, the chief purpose in the nuclear age must be to avert them,[18] a conclusion not accepted by the military for a considerable period of time. Again, the full meaning of mutual retaliation was not easily grasped in official circles. Not only was no distinction drawn as late as 1953 by the British Bomber Command between the use of nuclears as a first-strike force and as a second-strike retaliation after a Soviet nuclear attack,[19] but the doctrine of massive retaliation became the basis of official American policy in January 1954, in the very year the Russians revealed intercontinental bombing capability. While this was without doubt a political use of the concept aimed at creating uncertainty in the Russian mind on the exact terms upon which retaliation might occur, it stimulated powerful new criticisms of the strategic limits of deterrence. There emerged as a result a whole school of critics who were "would-be governmental advisers first and strategic theorists second."[20] Thus practice became the father of theory and of aspirants to the role of policy advisors.[21]

Using information not available to the public, these writers analyzed the technical problems of deterrence and, although differing in details, came to broadly similar conclusions about the importance of invulnerable retaliatory forces, the need for substantial capabilities of a large-scale shelter program in case deterrence should fail.

It is tempting to argue that the above theories, particularly Wohlsetter's analysis of the vulnerability of our strategic forces to surprise attack, were responsible for the dramatic shifts of the Kennedy administration.[22] Certainly the broad findings of their work seemed to be followed in the 1960s—the build-up of massive second-strike forces rather than reliance on minimum deterrence, the erection of strike options against an opponent's forces in the effort to create incentives against city-strikes, the emphasis upon the creation of substantial conventional forces for limited war situations and plans for extensive civil defense—all fitted the general proposals of the academic analysts.

Yet this is probably to overemphasize the role of theory. There were, after all, enormous pressures coming directly from the international system itself which were mainly responsible for the decisions to move in the directions indicated. For example, if decision-makers are faced with weapons which have the potential for complete destruction, they can be expected to follow the principle of over-insurance in numbers. Likewise, if the possibility of surprise attack exists, however remote, there will be pressures to adopt a worse case analysis and to spread the risks by building several types of deterrent systems. Hence the basic forces tended to work toward the decisions which were finally taken so that a sensible conclusion would seem to be that sophisticated theory provided a rationale which complemented environmental pressures.

At any rate, it is clear that when theory, however elegant or rational, departed from common sense and what was acceptable politically, it was theory which was abandoned and not implemented. The best example was the failure to persuade the nation to undertake a shelter program on a vast scale. Congress and the public proved recalcitrant and stubbornly resisted the pleadings of the specialists. In similar fashion, our European allies proved impervious to American pleas that deterrence would be enhanced by a substantial increase in their conventional military capacities. This reaction was a complex amalgam of political and economic assessment and owes little to the theory of deterrence. It was composed of fear that increased conventional capacity could lead to Soviet misperception concerning Western willingness to risk nuclear war, that a European increase might lead to an American reduction in forces committed to NATO, the economic costs of such a move and, finally, the lack of public support for increases. In the end, these political factors have proved stronger than any calculations based on abstract reason.

The key problems centering around deterrence all focus on the question of "stability." Just how stable *is* nuclear deterrence? It is a fact of our time that for most people it is taken for granted. We have, in a sense, become accustomed to living under the umbrella of the balance of terror, rather like people who live on the slopes of a volcano, perhaps glancing up now and again at the clouds of smoke which issue from the peak or listening with occasional uneasiness to the rumblings beneath, but by and large performing their daily round with something approaching equanimity. Nevertheless, the question should be asked and, if possible, answered.

The difficulty is, of course, that the answer is almost impossible to give with any degree of assurance because it rests on a host of interacting factors, such as the state of existing and prospective technology, the nature of conflict and bargaining and, above all, the political judgment of key decision-makers. All one can do, therefore, is to highlight a few key issues and, in the process, demonstrate the range and depth of the issues involved.

It should be said at once that expert opinion is seriously divided on all aspects of the issue. Of none is this more true than the technical reliability of nuclear forces. Although the deterrent has survived quite remarkable technical changes—manned bombers, liquid fuel rockets, solid fuel missiles, Polaris submarines, to name a few—the deductions drawn from these facts are by no means clear-cut. For one thing, many of these changes occurred during a period of substantial American superiority and it may be argued that, if these had occurred during a time of Russian predominance, deterrence might have collapsed. This is, of course, a political judgment, attributing a set of values to Russian leaders markedly different from our own. In many ways, it is a dubious argument to make and it is advanced here not for any intrinsic worth it might have but because such attributions did in fact lie behind the positions of those who argued the necessity for an overwhelming American lead in nuclear weapons.

There is another reason why we cannot use past technical change to argue for deterrence stability. Quite simply, it is because enormous efforts were made by the United States to overcome the instabilities which existed or were believed to exist. To put the matter crudely, deterrent "gaps" were anticipated in advance and measures were taken to eliminate these before they arose or, more conservatively, to see that they lasted for only a short period. There was, for example, a period in the 1950s when both the United States and Russia had large numbers of aircraft concentrated on a single base within the radius of a single bomb with response time too slow for reliable warning under ratios which favored the attacker by eight to one or more.[23] This vulnerability led to a serious attempt upon the very complex problems of designing protected second-strike forces capable of riding out an attack. The attempt apparently was successful but the growth of the Soviet missile force and the development of anti-ballistic missiles once again raised the stability issue in an acute form. A lengthy and detailed debate ensued led by able scientists on both sides of the vulnerability question.[24] No layman is in a position to evaluate the arguments developed, not because of their complexity but because those who argued for the vulnerability of nuclear forces did so on the basis of partly or wholly classified information.[25] The debate, in short, revolved around specific performance data which is not publicly available. What is clear from the discussion is that, under certain conditions, very large proportions of the Minuteman missile force could become vulnerable to an attack as missile accuracies improve and win the race against the hardening of silos. Those who wished to see these forces protected were really expressing a strong preference for a "mix" of deterrent forces—land-based missiles, bombers and submarine missiles—in order to complicate the task of a prospective attacker. Those who opposed ABM defenses were prepared in the last analysis to accept the deterrent value of submarines and bombers as sufficient even if substantial (though disputed) numbers of land-based missiles became vulnerable to attack. It is hard to escape the general conclusion that the "stability" of deterrence in the technological sense is a misleading notion. There are, in fact, different degrees of vulnerability which depend on the changing capabilities of the offense and the defense. Moreover, there is an intrinsic uncertainty about advancing technologies. It is a fact and not a theory that the United States was surprised by the speed with which the Soviet Union developed the atomic bomb, the hydrogen bomb as well as certain types of radars, and that in February 1953 a panel of distinguished scientists predicted that the Russians would not develop the ICBM before the late 1960s, when in fact they had it within the year. It is also a fact that informed scientists did not anticipate the development of MIRV's (multiple independently-targetable reentry vehicles), a new technology which, when deployed, will multiply warheads by a factor of three or four and by posing the danger of a first-strike, threaten to undermine existing forces to a substantial degree.[26]

Perhaps our recent experience suggests a moral: technology *by itself* cannot provide us with the necessary and sufficient conditions for stable deterrence. This is the "technological fallacy" and it contains within it serious dangers of deterrent collapse for two reasons. In times of seeming technical stability, it is an argument for doing nothing. Then when a technical change occurs, decision-makers are almost forced to remedy the situation by a technical response. Hence a vicious circle is created from which no escape exists. This is the inner logic of the technological approach and is the reason why we can assert with confidence that technology cannot supply the sufficient conditions for stable deterrence. True stability can never rest entirely on technical considerations but can only result from political decisions which attack the root causes of the arms race.

The concept of stable deterrence has other serious difficulties. The most fundamental of these is that the whole concept of nuclear retaliation rests at bottom on a threat to take irrational action. The point is well put by Herman Kahn: "In most deterrent situations, once deterrence has failed, it is natural to carry out the previously made warnings or threats of retaliation since that action will produce an absolute or net loss to the retaliator. Thus the threat of retaliation, in order to be believable, must depend on the potential irrationality of the retaliator."[27]

This will prove to be true whether one adopts an economic model of rationality in which the criteria of rationality encompass notions of efficient means to attain goals combined with estimates of consequences yielding maximum benefits at minimum costs or whether one uses the term "rational" to mean the opposite of actions taken out of shock or vengeance. In either use of the term the contemplated action is in fact irrational.

The severe logical difficulties which lie in the way of attempting to make rational what is at bottom irrational are clearly shown in the failure of efforts to present reasonable models of how limited strategic exchanges might be used as a possible strategy.[28] What the analysis reveals is that when nuclear weapons are used there are no clear boundaries or limitations which can be established. All are fundamentally arbitrary because such encounters are at bottom contests of resolve, of opposing wills. In such contests what each side does will be determined by what it calculates the other will do and what is required to break the will of the opponent.[29] But since the side which could demonstrate an irreversible trend would "win" the contest, there are inexorable pressures to go ever higher once strategic retaliation has begun. T. C. Schelling puts the point clearly when he says:

> The situation is fundamentally indeterminate as far as logic goes. There is no logical reason why two adversaries will not bleed each other to death, drop by drop, each continually feeling that if he can only hold out a little longer, the other is bound to give in. There is no assurance that both sides will not come to feel that everything is at stake in this critical test of endurance, that to yield is to acknowledge unconditional submissiveness.[30]

This logical indeterminacy applies not only to the use of strategic nuclear weapons capable of destroying whole cities but also to the use of tactical nuclear weapons, since behind these lie the massive bombs and the use of these latter could always be threatened if smaller nuclears were ever used. In short, there is only one threshold of violence which, if crossed, marks the boundary of rational action. That threshold is the first use of nuclear weapons.

This iron logic, which partakes of the very nature of strategic deterrence, explains why no commitment to use nuclears is irrevocable and why governments have not embraced policies involving their use as an automatic response to acts or threats of aggression.[31]

At this point it is necessary to make some distinctions which are crucial to a clear understanding of the degrees of stability which do exist. These distinctions rest on the fact that all threats to use nuclears are not equally irrational. In short, there are degrees of credibility which can be interpreted as conveying different degrees of stability. This involves difficult questions of political judgment and therefore the assertions which follow are highly tentative and not subject to rigorous demonstration. Nevertheless, the problem of credibility takes us into the realm in which practical political decisions are made, and it is these decisions which, in the final analysis, will play the greatest part in the actual workings of nuclear deterrence.

Briefly stated, there exists a curve of credibility which begins with defense of the homeland, descends to clearly defined spheres of influence or the territory of allies and then drops to near zero for the defense of other interests. It is possible to envisage, then, three broad categories of stakes which make sense of the actual practice of statesmen:[32] survival stakes (the homeland case), landslide stakes (which present the danger of a shift in the balance of power, and hence a loss of position in the hierarchy of states), and marginal stakes (which do not threaten a hierarchical shift). Thus we have a gradation of stakes in defense for which statesmen will be prepared to accept proportionate degrees of risk. Hence we find the late President Kennedy prepared to issue a threat of massive retaliation upon the Soviet Union if missiles from Cuba landed on American soil whereas the defense of our European allies is made to rest in the first instance on a substantial ability to resist with conventional arms. It is true that some nuclear threats were made in 1955 and 1958 over Quemoy and Matsu, but these were directed to a non-nuclear power (China) and occurred at a time of overwhelming American nuclear superiority. If the above analysis is correct we are not likely to see such nuclear threats made over marginal issues, now that we are well along in the age of mutual deterrence.

The concept of a hierarchy of stakes and risks also enables us to explain the outcomes of some of the crises which have plagued the international system. To apply these ideas we must first grasp the fact that it is necessary to compare the *relative* size of the stakes for the contestants and their ability to bring to bear conventional military power. For example, in Hungary the stakes for the United States were marginal as compared to those for the Soviet Union. The American government, therefore, could not have made a credible nuclear threat, even though it did have a superiority in such weapons.[33] The Soviet Union felt free to use its conventional military power to crush the uprising. The exact contrary was the case in the Cuban Missile Crisis, where a Russian move in an American sphere of influence left the United States free to use the pressure of its air and naval superiority to force a Soviet backdown. In order to escape without a diplomatic defeat, the Russians would have had to risk making nuclear threats on a matter of marginal importance, thus endangering their survival. This they wisely refused to do.

The difficulty in making nuclear threats credible in the era of mutual deterrence also explains why the art of brinkmanship as practiced by John Foster Dulles has faded from the scene and, above all, why states began to stress the importance of "flexible response," a euphemism for raising the nuclear threshold by increasing one's conventional military capacity.

The actual practice of statesmen, therefore, has tended to depart from the elaborate and sophisticated suggestions of the deterrence theorists. Strategies of irrational threats *might* not work and the opponent *might* make the first fatal move. So the statesmen seem to have decided that these ideas, while interesting, should not be put to the test since, if they proved mistaken, the mistake would be fatal. Instead, they have evolved rules out of the dangerous experiences through which the world has passed: avoid direct confrontation; no limited war between nuclear states; respect the hegemony of clearly established spheres of influence; and keep the nuclear threshold as high as is practicable. These rules are unwritten. Like all rules they could be violated deliberately or by mistake. They are essentially short-term responses to the dangers posed by nuclear weapons. They do not fully circumvent those dangers even in the short run, but they do remind us that the sense of prudence in the minds of statesmen is the best safeguard we have at this juncture in history.

These rules of prudence do not protect us from the long-term dangers inherent in nuclear deterrence.[34] As long ago as 1955, Sir Winston Churchill reminded us that "the deterrent does not cover the case of lunatics or dictators in the mood of Hitler when he found himself in his final dugout. This is a blank." Indeed it is, and it is likely to remain an enormous gap in the security of deterrence for a very long time to come.

Other dangers do exist. Despite the hotline or the failsafe mechanisms which are built in to the weapons, technical accidents could occur.[35] Communications with Polaris submarines are notoriously difficult and efforts to warn surface ships have failed in an actual emergency.[36] Nor do we have any information on Soviet procedures in these matters—they may be better than ours or worse, but in any case a breakdown could occur.

Besides, a miscalculation could occur over the size of an opponent's stake in a conflict or through fear of a surprise attack during a period of technological change when transitory superiorities might coincide with a grave crisis. All these point to the need not only to refine safety precautions of all sorts and to maintain the invulnerability of weapons, but to tackle the larger issues of controlling the arms race and to develop institutions which reflect the general interests of mankind in the avoidance of war and the preservation of peace.

How can this be done? How do we move from the state of partially controlled tension, which is of the essence in nuclear deterrence, to a condition of true peace? The task will be long and difficult, but the first step is to realize that apathy and blind confidence in the stability of nuclear deterrence are the most intransigent obstacles to a resolution of the dilemma we confront. The second task is to face the political and technical facts boldly, without fudging the issues. These facts are two-fold: on the one hand, nuclear weapons have kept a kind of peace through terror and they will *not* be given up by the great powers, at least in the foreseeable future; on the other hand, there are serious instabilities in the present system and it cannot be expected to last indefinitely without a serious breakdown. These two propositions tell us that mankind is, therefore, caught on the horns of a dilemma and escape will not be easy.[37]

Traditional theory emphasizes a solution based on disarmament culminating in the establishment of a world authority with a monopoly of power such that aggressor states would not dare challenge it.[38]

This position stems directly from the main Western legal tradition which emphasizes the attributes of the nation-state, particularly the monopoly of force, and extends these by analogy to the international system. Leonard Beaton has offered a major critique of this tradition and formulated a stimulating and imaginative alternative.[39]

Beaton's critique is based on assertions concerning the political reactions of the great powers to the nuclear dilemma. He argues that the abolition of nuclear forces is not negotiable, that the great powers will resist domination by a central legal institution, that such an institution could not enforce law on the great powers (and if it tried to do so would be introducing the idea of waging war in order to abolish war) and that responsibility for enforcement must rest on the ‚states themselves.[40] In short, his argument is that if the major states want a war, no international security system could stop it and the great powers will insist on maintaining their national security systems to meet possible major challenges. The first step, therefore, is to recognize these realities and to build common institutions on the limited willingness of states to recognize common interests in international security. The basic common interest is that the present structure of power cannot last indefinitely. It contains within itself sources of instability which require common action. The major difficulty is, of course, that governments believe in the existence of a stable balance of terror and resist thinking about the long-term problems of instability, in direct contrast to the pressure of public opinion for world disarmament. This creates the serious danger that no practical steps will be taken to reduce instabilities, while public opinion is soothed by essentially unattainable schemes for general and complete disarmament.

What is needed is a conscious attempt to build on international security authority which would not undermine existing sources of security, but would minimize the dangers of accident and miscalculation, control the evolution of weapons and eventually lead to a structure for the peaceful settlement of disputes.[41] Such an authority must show itself capable of dealing with genuine problems, the first of which is a thorough "knowledge and understanding of the armed forces of the states of the world and the security policies these have been designed to serve."[42] This step could undercut generalized fears of insecurity which otherwise might lead to a cycle of increased defense expenditure. In short, ignorance breeds fear and insecurity, whereas security begins with knowledge.[43] Detailed examination of defense policies will lead to the acceptance of military activities as reasonable or to the reverse conclusion if these cannot withstand rational examination. Present political antagonisms are such that in its initial stages such an examination of defense policies would probably begin with wild exaggerations and extreme accusations by the parties. The hope would be that gradually the common interest in reasonable security policies would prevail.

The obvious place to begin such a process would be the United Nations and the suggestion is that there be created a Defense Committee of the Security Council to hear evidence and assess the implications of the forces that exist and might be created.[44] In this way some consensus over security policy might develop. A professional staff would be required to make policy studies and formulate proposals. Thus a political context would be created which could lead to informal measures of arms control and provide reassurance to medium and small states. The sense of being in a growing system would help offset pressures for heavy weapons expenditure and nuclear proliferation. A link would thus be formed between the actual security policies of states and the general interest of all states in world security.

Restraint on the expansion of existing nuclear forces, advances in ballistic missile technology, the control of nuclear proliferation—all require continuous dialogue and negotiation. Initially governments will resist discussions of their plans and control systems, but they have a basic interest in secure knowledge of the strategic thinking of their rivals and hence a mutual interest in good intelligence. Only gradually will such a process build confidence and consensus. For a very long time governments will insist that no steps be taken which threaten their ultimate control over their own forces. There is, in short, both a national and a world security interest and any international security organization must reflect this fact. National governments will commit forces to such an organization only if their security objectives are achieved by it and if they can do so under national control so that if the two interests conflict they can protect themselves by withdrawal.

The great powers might, however, be prepared to assign a portion of their Polaris submarine fleet to the management of an international authority at some point in the above process with the proviso that it could not be used without the approval of the great powers and that it could be returned to national control under certain conditions. No fears of domination by a central authority would be aroused but experience would be gained in operating institutions in the common interest. In some such way a gradual transfer of authority to international peace-keeping institutions could become a reality. Eventually such a force might come to be operated entirely by the world organizations. In some similar way, limited forces might be assigned specific peace-keeping tasks followed by a like shift of authority. At any rate, the principle is clear: no sudden shift from national strategies to a grand design is likely to occur. If it occurs, it will only be by experimental means with the assumption of responsibility by a world organization based on consensus and proved effectiveness. Beaton puts the matter well when he says:

> The powers . . . are now organized on a sovereign basis with international arrangements. They could go over to an international system with sovereign arrangements with no essential alteration in their present capacity to defend themselves and their allies. But they could create the technical and military context and perhaps the political conditions in which their common servants could achieve the common object of severely limiting or even abolishing war which may otherwise elude them.[45]

The distance between the kind of imaginative attack on the security dilemma proposed by Beaton and the actual practice of states is enormous. Attempts to control the missile race have proceeded at a snail's pace. The euphoria which heralded the signing of the first Strategic Arms Limitation agreement in 1972 has been dissipated. The accords at Vladivostock which set extremely high quantitative levels for the super-powers have not, at the time of writing, been followed up by further progress. Meanwhile technology has continued its remorseless advance: more accurate guidance systems, improved versions of MIRV missiles and a longer-range submarine system (Trident), a new version of the cruise missile and a host of precision-guided conventional weapons, to name but a few developments. Some of these weapons carry potential threats to land-based missile forces. Others, like the cruise missile, hold the potential for extending enormously the capabilities of bombing aircraft. Whether the overall effect of these new weapons will be to undermine existing second-strike capabilities or merely complicate the deterrence function is by no means clear. Nor is it yet evident what the responses of the super-powers will be to these costly and complex additions to their armories. If the past is any guide, they are likely to wait until the consequences of the new technologies are clearer before deciding on how to deal with them. Some unilateral measures, such as shifting from major reliance on land-based missiles to bombers and ballistic submarines, might downgrade temptations for first-strike action. Such a shift would be costly but probably inevitable unless significant breakthroughs can be made in the dialogue between the two giants. Meanwhile, it is clear that some of the newer developments resist monitoring by unilateral means and, indeed, may demand inspection which is quite intrusive. If all this were not ominous enough, the world is also faced with the dangers implicit in the spread of nuclear technology and a staggering increase in the sale of quite sophisticated conventional weapons to third world countries.[46] The ability of the super-powers to control these last two dangerous trends is limited, not just by the fact of their own competition but by their inadequate means of influence and by the potential demands of third parties. By increasingly strenuous efforts they may be able to prevent major conflicts between themselves but the elements needed to transcend their rivalries for common purposes do not seem to be present in sufficient degree.[47] Technology and great power competition are in the saddle and ride mankind.

Will the great powers embark on a politically imaginative course of action or will they drift along on the present powerful currents of technological change and political competition, content with temporary arrangements aimed at short-term answers to their security dilemmas? No one can say with any degree of assurance although the latter paths seems more likely. What we know is that the cost of deterrence and defense is extremely high in economic and human terms and that the risks are enormous. It seems highly unlikely either that the costs will decline or that even tremendous exertions will return states to the pre-nuclear situation in which it was believed that reasonable security could be attained by purely national means. Sovereignty, in the sense of independent action, really no longer exists, even for a super-power, since it is exercised in a world in which other states have the ability to destroy it. It is a strange and truncated sovereignty by which a state is forced to spend 100 billions a year under the pressure of a neighbor's action, following which the only security obtained is that provided by the mutuality of destruction.

Yet this is the situation in which we find ourselves and it is worth remembering that, while the techniques which have produced the instruments that provide the present truce of terror are based on science and technology, the basic facts which lead to this misuse of knowledge are ethical choices. We cannot remind ourselves too often that it is men's values, and ultimately even their ethical values, which are the basic causes of threats to peace. For it is these values which men, organized in nation-states, are prepared to defend by force if need be. War and strategy simply reflect the fact that men are prepared at some point to defend or advance their interests by force and that they are not yet ready to surrender force as an ultimate sanction. They have carried this demand to the point where it threatens them with extinction. Hence the "peace" which obtains is the transitory condition we call the balance of terror and not the peace which is the product of a world order stemming from a world community of mankind. The erection of a system of peaceful change strong enough and stable enough to withstand the demands which will inevitably be placed upon it is by far the most difficult task ever tackled by human beings. All we can know for certain is that no long-term alternative exists. We cannot rely for much longer on the use of armed force and the balance of power for our security. Man must create a political system which takes account of the facts of security in the nuclear age if he wishes to escape destruction on a scale which defies imagination. Old habits and fears combined with the momentum of established structures of power carry us along the older pathways of force, strategy and politics. Interest and duty alike demand new departures.

9
Rival Explanations in International Relations

The great scientist and mathematician Poincaré once remarked scornfully of the study of sociology: "most methods; least results." The comment, while perhaps unduly patronizing, does represent a commonly held view of attempts at scientific explanation in human affairs. Scholars have added weight to this general opinion by seemingly endless and inconclusive debates over the proper approach to method, often to the exclusion of actual efforts to solve concrete problems. The study of international relations has had its own disputes over the nature of explanation and no book which purports to deal with the state of the discipline can ignore the issue raised in these debates.

The reason is simple: both students who seek to learn about the subject and statesmen who make policies which involve the destiny of millions of citizens must be able to decide between explanations which are valid and those which are not. Indeed, we cannot even communicate without some form of theory, much less engage in critical debate about the meaning of events. In short, we are all theoreticians and the only issue is what kinds of theories should we adopt to guide us in our attempts to understand the subject matter. We must therefore deal with the vexing questions of what we know and how we know what is claimed as knowledge.

In the process, a complex set of questions is raised which tends to polarize opinion and divide people into warring camps. This is doubly unfortunate since such polarization of views tends to impede the search for truth and to hide the fact that rival attempts at explanation often contain a good deal more in common than may appear at first sight. The end result is a net loss to the scholarly community and to those who make decisions in the actual arena of world politics.

Our procedure will be to examine the nature of historical explanation and then go on to examine the views of a critic of scientific explanation—Hedley Bull. We shall then summarize the advantages and limitations of the two approaches in as concise and objective an appraisal as we can achieve.

It is vital to recognize in the first place that no hard and fast line can be drawn between history and science with respect to method. Both approach their subject in the following way: examination of the data; formulation of an explanatory hypothesis; analysis of the consequences of the hypothesis and test of these consequences against additional data.

There are of course significant differences, differences which stem not from the subject but from the focus of interest of the analyst. The scientist is interested in facts as a means to the discovery of general laws. The historian's focus is upon particular facts and to this end he uses generalizations to explain the case at hand. The generalizations which the historian makes the most use of are not the universal laws which form the basis of science but for the most part are transitory regularities rooted in temporally restricted technological or institutional patterns. In short, the historian works with general statements of limited scope, statements which are valid only for particular periods and particular conditions.[1]

This focus on particular time periods, specific incidents and specific actors, a focus generally shared by most practicing historians, has certain obvious limitations. An account based on particular conditions cannot, for example, be used for predictive purposes nor can it easily be used to help us understand the present. To attain these purposes it is necessary to go beyond common-sense analysis to a more rigorous analytical framework. If the data are plentiful and if they lend themselves to more rigorous definition, the practitioner of scientific method can sometimes provide us with additional insights. By comparing sets of data he can tell us for example the extent to which alliance partners fulfilled their commitments and he can provide evidence that while alliances in the nineteenth century seem to have acted as restraints on war, the opposite is true for the twentieth century.[2] Thus the two approaches are found to complement one another in significant ways.

It is true, of course, that any approach can be distorted or abused by its practitioners. Enormous efforts at analysis may be produced in order to demonstrate obvious and relatively insignificant incidents. For example, the purposes of research are not advanced noticeably by elaborate techniques designed to demonstrate that during the Suez crisis hostile signals increased in the October–

November period and declined thereafter.[3] Sophistication in method can be a mask which covers a paucity of good theoretical ideas.[4] Worse, exasperation and even contempt can develop as a result and needed cooperation between historians and social scientists can suffer as a consequence. Methodology is no substitute for creative ideas.

History can also produce negative reactions if its custodians overemphasize description rather than interpretation, if the concepts used are not defined carefully and if the accumulation of facts becomes an end in itself. In the hands of a writer with insight and the willingness to engage in comparative analysis, however, the results can be impressive and stimulating.[5] Such a task ranging over three centuries can only be undertaken by someone steeped in the primary sources and acquainted with detailed research. It would be far beyond the scholarly capacity of persons specializing in the social science aspects of the subject. In short, a natural division of labor exists which is a necessary condition for the advance of understanding. States did not in fact pursue their interests in the same way over the centuries and the reasons why this is so form an essential aspect of comprehending the processes of change. Once these processes are analyzed for us by the historian it may then be possible to explain such changes by comparing them to analogous developments studied by students in sociology, anthropology or social psychology. The reverse procedure, however, is full of grave dangers since the enquirer is not equipped with the detailed knowledge necessary to detect when changing conditions nullify the propositions which are being tested. Thus, the requirement for cumulative progress is the same in both cases: intense and close collaboration by historians and social scientists.

At this juncture it is necessary for us to examine in more detail the structure of historical explanation. For by doing so, we can better appreciate some of its strengths and limitations.

The historian, if given adequate documentation, can, in principle and sometimes in practice, produce an account which contains the necessary and sufficient conditions for an event or a policy. This may seem to be too sweeping a claim but it can be defended with considerable force. To defend it, however, we must be clear about what we demand of an explanation. If we believe that true or adequate explanation consists only in our ability to deduce an event from a general law or a set of such laws, then neither history nor any of the social sciences could produce an adequate explanation of any reasonably complex event or, at least, one which went much beyond a simple stimulus-response activity.

But, in fact, the demand for deduction from general laws, as a total procedure, is much too restrictive. If, on the other hand, we set a less demanding standard and accept as adequate a coherence theory of explanation, we can often produce accounts which come very close to producing the necessary and sufficient conditions of an event.

Now, what do we mean by a coherence account of an event? We mean basically a set of two factual propositions which, linked and taken together, with interpretative hypotheses, constitute a system in which the facts and hypotheses provide mutual support for each other.

The truth of *particular* propositions used in the set is a question of relationship to the actual facts. The adequacy of the *total set* is determined by the adequacy of the fit between the total set and the *event* to be explained. In order to judge the adequacy of a particular system three criteria are used: *comprehensiveness, consistency* and *cohesiveness*. By comprehensiveness is meant the extent to which the system explains a range of facts going to explain the event. By consistency we mean simply that the propositions which go to make up the system must not contradict one another according to the accepted rules of logic. By cohesiveness is meant interdependence, the idea of mutual implication, such that if the truth status of a fact were different, the adequacy of the whole set would be affected.[6]

Such an approach to explanation in history accords very closely with the actual practices of historians in the ongoing search for adequate accounts of events. It describes a process, the gradual buildup of a framework or picture in which data are selected, used or discarded as the framework is formed and the data are enlarged and as hypotheses connecting the facts are asserted, modified or discarded in their turn. In such a process the key issue is always the degree to which the total set conforms to a pattern which best fits the available data. At any given moment the set of facts and hypotheses is an approximation of the truth in the light of available evidence. In the case of some events, the evidence may be so slight that the rational warrant for asserting the plausibility of the account may be highly tentative. In other cases, the volume and quality of the evidence may be so large, and the fit of the overall set so accurate, that it can be asserted that a "complete" explanation has been given. "Complete" here means that the necessary and sufficient conditions of the event have been brought together in a coherent manner such that it neither contradicts known empirical facts nor goes against general laws based on previous experience. It also implies that "completeness" is a relative term subject to the availability of evidence and to the known fact that any explanation of whatever kind is subject to revisability in the light of new facts or new theoretical understanding. In short, the "completeness" of a coherence account of a historical event is a function of available evidence and is subject to modification as understanding and inquiry proceed. It is "complete" only in the sense of being a more or less close approach to explanation in the light of existing known facts and our understanding of them.

A great deal of misunderstanding arises because at this point one can ask: "Can't we always ask another 'why' question of any given account?" The answer is: "Of course, but most of these 'why' questions are questions which raise issues that are *not* in the province of the historian." We can, for example, ask: "Why did this particular motive exist for a British or German statesman?" At one level this is a historical question to be answered in the light of that person's purposes. At another level it is a question for psychology, for the scientific study of the mental processes which derive from the dynamics of human personality and needs. This implies a division of labor between disciplines and a clear understanding of what questions are legitimate to ask and what questions are not.

The fact that the core of historical explanation consists of a coherence-type of analysis casts a great deal of light on the disputes which rage over the logical structure of such explanation. These disputes revolve around such questions as whether historical narratives rest on a series of general laws (explicitly or implicitly), a number of limited laws, or on purely empirical propositions of the common-sense type in which either rules or reasons are cited to explain actions.[7]

The coherence account is able to give an answer to most of the issues raised in these analyses without strain or embarrassment of any sort. Its general response is: a particular explanation based on the coherence approach can accommodate any combination of general and/or limited laws together with any number of particular empirical propositions. The exact specification of the items making up the total set will vary from case to case depending on the state of the evidence available and the existing state of scientific knowledge. In general terms there will tend to be at present very few general laws (most of them being physical laws and therefore only implicitly referred to); very often limited regularities holding for a particular time period or particular aspect of the events will appear in the set (usually referring to technological possibilities or economic constraints); the main burden of supplying connecting links between facts will tend to be borne by empirical propositions derived from common-sense knowledge. In short, the exact logical structure of coherence accounts cannot be described in general terms but is always case specific.

Nor is a coherence account of a complex historical event in

danger of being superseded by an account based on general laws only. There are several reasons why this is so. In the first place, while we may possess some *general* laws which cover a particular aspect of events (economic, social or psychological) these are few in number and do not suffice to explain the bulk of historical happenings. Secondly, even if such laws existed or could be developed in greater numbers (which may very well be the future situation), such laws hold only under specified conditions *and* are statistical in nature, i.e., they hold only in a specified percentage of cases. Now, it is precisely the task of the historian to examine (a) the particular conditions under which generalizations (of any type or extent) obtain *and/or* (b) to explain why, in a particular case, the law concerned did *not* in fact hold. Thirdly, for most historical events we would find that a *combination* of uniformities and particularized empirical hypotheses would be required to present an intelligible explanation. That is, we would have to construct a web of meaning consisting of clusters of laws and particular hypotheses, *each set tending to be unique to the case at hand.* This last remark should not be taken to prejudge the case as to whether two or more sets dealing with a similar class of events might or might not be linked by a still higher level generalization. This is a question, not of philosophical argument, but of empirical fact. Thus, one could have a number of case studies of particular crises consisting of facts linked by empirical hypotheses and these might then be explained by a number of limited laws or regularities.[8] Such a limited set of regularities is specifically historical in the precise sense that the regularities hold only for a specific time period. They do not hold as stated for either an earlier or later period. These regularities might, however, be derivable from a still higher level generalization relating for example to some aspect of conflict analysis. If so, the generalization of which they were a series of instances would in all likelihood be propositions of sociology or social psychology and hence not historical in nature. At this point arguments about historical explanation are really arguments about the nature of reality. All that we can say is that, in the light of our present knowledge, no universal historical propositions (i.e., propositions which are true in every case) are known to exist and that the statistical generalizations which do exist tend to cover fairly limited periods of time or a narrow range of events. If more general propositions do exist, they are likely to consist of fairly abstract propositions based upon totally different levels of analysis and meaning.[9] If developed, they might be applied to a series of events or policies in history and thus produce a new perspective and hence a new understanding. That is to say, we would then attach a new meaning to certain facts and situations.

This schematic account of the logical structure of historical explanation should make clear why, given a reasonable body of evidence, it is often easier to produce a satisfactory historical explanation than it is to construct a meaning for historical events based on behavioral laws and why prediction in history by any techniques whatever is, to say the least, a highly dubious enterprise.

The historian's task, difficult as it is, begins with a given consequence or result. It is an explanation backwards in time and because the historian knows at least in a rough way the results or consequences, he can often tease out the network of causation in a surprisingly complete fashion. The problem of prediction is another matter entirely. Here there are at least four major impediments:

(1) the existence of a complex of *interrelated* laws both general and limited;

(2) the rise of new, independent structures or conditions;

(3) the fact that known laws are statistical in nature and therefore hold in only a certain percentage of cases;

(4) the probable existence of unknown laws (which in the historian's case are often revealed *after* the fact).

Our present knowledge rarely permits us to say in what way a particular set of laws will interact with another set. Hence, we find that "accidents" occur in history, that is to say there occurs the unanticipated crossing of two or more causal chains. Moreover, we are always being surprised by the appearance of new, novel structures or conditions. This is either the result of the aforementioned "accidents" or hidden implications in a single causal sequence which develops its own autonomous movement. There is also of course the fact that the regularities observed hold only in a statistical way and so we cannot predict *single* events even in the case of laws which are based upon large numbers of events (such as life-insurance tables or road accidents). Finally, it is an observed fact that, after events have occurred, we are almost always able to detect hitherto unsuspected conditions or gradations of known conditions or even previously unknown regularities.

The combined effect of these four factors explains why the hope of prediction remains a chimera. All such efforts are really either simple exponential extensions of existing trends into the future or are an arbitrary selection of a few assumptions shaped into a possible future scenario. Either method *might*, purely by chance, produce a correct prediction but the likelihoods are not high. Hence the bogey of determinism, so eloquently expressed by Sir Isaiah Berlin,[10] that we might some day get "a series of natural laws connecting, at one end, the biological and physiological states and processes of human beings, with at the other, the equally observable patterns of their conduct ... and hence predict the publicly observable behavior of men," turns out to be a totally misguided fear. Such a fear is groundless, not merely because such a science of human behavior does not exist (some day it might) but because, even if it did, it would only form a small fraction of what happens in history. The historical process, for the reasons cited, cannot be made the subject of a predictive process except for a very narrow range of events and for a restricted time period. The bulk of it escapes our predictive grasp.

It is quite otherwise with our understanding of what actually has happened in history. Though passages of doubt remain for very large tracts of time and for many events, we can supply for some cases a detailed explanation which resembles in many respects a fully deterministic account. For here we *know* the consequences and because we have access to national archives we often have a very complete account of precisely how men acted to produce the results they did. Our knowledge of historical events is, indeed, often embarrassed by superabundance so that it takes a generation or more of historians to assimilate the data and to produce their accounts.

So far these claims for the usefulness and logical respectability of historical explanation have been couched in general terms. Can we cite some practical examples? The answer is "yes." For example, the student who wishes to understand how World War I came about or how policies leading to World War II were developed can do so. In the former case he can read detailed analyses, the fruit of more than fifty years of work by hundreds of scholars who have sifted and weighed the evidence.[11] In the case of the latter, he can see how the process of sifting and distillation is proceeding on specific problems and interpretations, the *end result* of which will be a coherent account of why and how the second world war accrued.[12]

In contrast to these specific studies of how particular wars occurred, attempts to discover significant and fruitful generalizations which hold for wars in general or for particular types of wars have so far not been notably successful.[13] Why should this be? A general answer is because the complex of factors which led to war varied enormously from case to case so that the onset of a particular conflict cannot be deduced from a generalization or series of them, at least in the present state of our knowledge of the phenomena.

The case is quite otherwise with our attempts to understand how a specific conflict arose. Here we can describe in detail exactly how a period of armed peace after 1871 gradually changed into a pre-war period about 1900 due to several interacting factors:[14] the revolution in the technology of war placing an emphasis on the speed and superiority of the offensive, the growing inflexibility of alliances due to specific sources of mistrust, rapid and increasing changes in the relative strengths of the great powers, the rise of separatist and uncontrollable nationalist movements, the occurrence of a series of crises and limited conflicts, the whole tending to produce an all but universal readiness among decision-makers to let events take their course. In the end, war came to be preferred to the strain of recurring crises in an armed and uneasy peace. That is to say we can describe how particular factors and the decisions relating to these interacted in a manner which led to decisions for war in 1914. These conclusions do not apply, however, to other conflicts in exactly the same manner because general factors such as the effects of particular weapons technologies, the relative power of the potential antagonists and a host of other conditions were peculiar to the period in question.

In order to bring out the difficulties of establishing significant generalizations which extend over long periods of time, consider for a moment the deterrent effects of weapons on decisions for war. Contrast for example the pre-1914 situation with the deterrent facts which now confront the great powers. In the former case, technology placed a premium on such factors as numbers of men and weapons, the need to gear plans for war to mobilization and getting in the first blow if possible. Above all, it was still possible in 1914 to believe that a general war could be won at bearable cost. In the 1970s the situation has changed radically. Nuclear weapons have placed a premium on readiness but surprise attack cannot prevent a retaliatory blow of unbelievable proportions. Entire societies can be virtually annihilated in minutes and—most important of all—no one can make a convincing case for the argument that a general war can be won at bearable cost. Hence, the same generalizations concerning the deterrent effect of weapons cannot be applied to the two time periods in question. Deterrence to war did exist in both cases but the conditions under which it operated in the period 1900–1914 and the range of actors for which it was effective differed in profound and far-reaching ways from the present time.

If comparisons were made in detail between other major components of the international system, one would discover equally significant differences between the two periods in question. One would find for example that alliances played a different part in the story and operated in different ways and that the relative size and relationships among the great powers were also very different. The end result is that in order to present an accurate account of events it would be necessary to pinpoint the time when conditions changed to such an extent that generalizations need to be modified or new hypotheses devised to explain new relationships among the data. Thus, to take the deterrence example, we would find that the period before 1914, while differing in some respects, bears a much closer resemblance to the pre-1939 period than the post-nuclear era. Generalizations about conventional-style deterrence, with some modifications, could be applied to the first two periods but these could not explain the behavior of states for the years since the development of the hydrogen bomb.

The general analysis of historical explanation or outline above suggests that there are factors operating in history which pose formidable problems for theorists. There are in fact elements of contingency, irrationality and fortuituous behavior which will always prevent the development of a complete theory of international relations—or any other series of historical events for that matter. In addition, any theoretical analysis, whether historical or scientific, may be invalidated by factors which are present without our knowledge and which therefore have consequences which we cannot predict. There are thus sharp theoretical limits to our understanding and a clear recognition of these should curb extravagant claims that are sometimes made on behalf of theory. These limits apply to any type of analysis. They fall with equal severity upon the type of common-sense explanation so characteristic of history and the more abstract realm of scientific analysis.

Let us now turn to a more specific series of issues relating to scientific explanation in international relations. In particular we shall examine the criticisms offered by Hedley Bull.[15]

The case made by Hedley Bull for what he terms the "classical" approach to international theory and the strictures which he brings to bear upon the scientific approach constitute a curious compound of keen insight, half-truths and serious methodological errors. It is important that the strengths and the shortcomings of his critique be carefully assessed, not only in the interests of accuracy but because, if his arguments are correct, there is a sharp dichotomy between the classical and scientific approaches to the subject, which confronts us with a sharp choice of method and also because the dispute threatens to divide the profession into warring camps. Such a development would be not only regrettable but positively harmful, all the more so because it is in fact unnecessary and based on a profound misunderstanding about the very nature of scientific investigation and, indeed, the structure of scientific theories.

A critical examination of Bull's case is made difficult by the fact that it is hedged about with a plenitude of disclaimers and qualifications, but we take it that he wishes to assert something like the following series of propositions: (1) the scientific approach has contributed little and is likely to contribute very little to the study of international relations; (2) by confining themselves to what can be logically and mathematically proved or verified according to strict procedures, the practitioners of the scientific approach are denying themselves the only instruments at present available for coming to grips with the substance of the subject since, presumably, they must abstain from "intuitive guesses," "wisdom literature" and the "capacity for judgment" appropriate to moral questions and the testing of hypotheses; (3) the subject matter of international relations is "essentially intractable" because of its protean nature, the existence of an unmanageable number of variables, the resistance of the material to controlled experiment and the fact that theories and events are related not only as subject and object but also as cause and effect so that the theories contribute to their own verification and falsification; (4) a great disservice is done to theory by conceiving of it as the construction of models. There is no model, conceived of as a deductive system of axioms and theorems, which could not just as well be expressed as an empirical generalization. Model builders attribute to their models a connection with reality they do not have and then distort these by importing into the model additional assumptions in the guise of logical axioms. They are also guilty, according to Bull's indictment, of substituting methodological tools and the question, "Are the models useful or not?" for the assertion of propositions about the world and the questions "Are they true or not?", thus obscuring the issues of an empirical test. Finally, they have a fetish for measurement which may ignore relevant differences between phenomena or which may impute to what has been counted a significance it does not have.

Reasonable men may differ on the question whether the scientific approach has contributed much or little to the present study of the subject but when Bull goes on to say it is likely to contribute little in the future, he is indulging in an attempt at arbitrary legislation. If he presents examples of existing theories to substantiate the first part of his assertion, the answer to him must be that, although he may have seen inadequate theories, the fundamental problem is how we justify the theoretical enterprise. One promising method of doing so is the scientific approach, which can be used to discover significant correlations and to test existing hypotheses.

The practitioners of the scientific approach must have been surprised to learn that their approach denies them either intuitive guesses or the exercise of judgment. The plain fact is that the great scientists have all practiced intuition, if by that term we mean "a sudden enlightenment" or "a clarifying idea which springs into the consciousness."[16] The list of testimonies to the importance of intuition includes such distinguished investigators as Poincaré, Kropotkin, Von Helmholtz, Darwin and Einstein. The latter's statement on the subject was pungent and to the point: "The really valuable factor [in scientific investigation] is intuition."[17] In short, despite the fact that our world is of baffling complexity, certain kinds of regularities have been discovered by men of genius following upon immersion in the data and by means of an intuitive "leap."[18] Intuition, far from being denied the man of science, is central to his success.

The main issue is joined with Bull, however, at another level of argument altogether, namely, the proper procedure by which we establish statements which purport to convey knowledge. On this question Bull takes the position that the classical approach, defined as the derivation of theory from philosophy, history and law is best if terms are defined, logical canons of procedure are followed and assumptions made explicit. This approach is scientific, according to Bull, in the sense of being a coherent, precise and orderly body of knowledge and in the sense that it is consistent with the philosophical foundations of modern science.

Now it should be said at once that no advocate of the scientific approach could object to this argument *so far as it goes*. His reply is simply that it does not go far enough. Bull's approach *is* capable of providing us with the all-important inductive generalizations which are the primary step in theory construction. At this point, however, we must then ask: "How can we discriminate among hypotheses in order to discover which of them are essential to the theoretical task?"

The key word, in short, for Bull as for the rest of us, is "coherent." How precisely can he determine that his inductive hypotheses are, in fact, coherent? This means that they must be shown to be related in such a way that they are not inconsistent or incompatible with one another. The most effective way of doing this is to formulate a hypothetico-deductive system which will reveal whether some of the hypotheses are incompatible or whether some are equivalent and therefore deducible from others. In short, what is needed is a *model* which enables us to weed out unnecessary hypotheses and to clarify what must be done to provide partial confirmation or rejection.

When Bull states that a model is made up of deductive systems of axioms and theorems and that these could just as well be expressed as empirical generalizations, he asserts what is not, in fact, the case. No model is made up of logical axioms but, rather, of empirical propositions. The mathematical and logical aspects of the model simply concern the legitimate transformation rules which govern the model. The fact that a model is made up of empirical generalizations does not mean, as Bull apparently believes, that the model is itself an empirical generalization or that the latter can be substituted for it. This is a category mistake since the class of empirical statements is not itself an empirical statement.

Bull is equally in error when he asserts that the scientific approach substitutes the question, "Are the models *useful* or not?" for assertions about the empirical world and the question, "Are they true or not?" The facts of the matter are that logicians and philosophers of science have recognized for some time that there is no criterion of truth outside formalized languages.[19]

Instead, science substitutes the concept of "degrees of confirmation," which depends upon the evidence and which therefore ranges from high certainty to very low probability. The most efficient way to arrive at testable hypotheses is by way of their location in a hypothetico-deductive system.[20] Such a system will enable us to show that some of the statements are directly confirmed or disproved and, if the former, that the higher level hypotheses are indirectly confirmed. Those theories which prove to be useful are then put at a high premium.

Bull's denunciation of measurement which may "ignore relevant differences between phenomena" or "imputes a significance to what has been counted which it does not have" can be dismissed as special pleading. A correct measurement is by definition one which does not ignore relevant differences. If a measurement does ignore such differences, it is a useless form of measurement. A similar comment can be made on conclusions which attribute false significance to the data being measured. Faulty procedures are faulty procedures, no matter what the rubric under which they are pursued or whoever their author might happen to be. It is therefore irrelevant to the issue at hand that certain distinguished advocates of the scientific approach have or have not made such errors and it only clouds the problem to contest or to uphold Bull's assertions in this connection.

The real issue, therefore, is not whether mistakes have been made in the task of measurement but how to improve our present inadequate techniques of measurement. It simply will not do to plead that we deal with unique phenomena, since any particular event whatsoever is unique in some respect,[21] or that we are faced with data resistant to controlled experiment, since this is characteristic of certain of the natural sciences, or that our material changes even as we observe it, for this too is characteristic of nature as well as all social phenomena.[22] The truly formidable obstacles to theory construction lie elsewhere, chiefly in the fundamental fact that we are often simply unaware of the true nature of the data we are attempting to describe and analyze. This is due to a variety of factors—simple lack of information, the hiding or deliberate falsifi-cation of facts, the absence of adequate definition and classification, and the scarcity of good theoretical ideas. As long as this condition prevails, not only "classical" types of explanation but the most thoroughgoing model will not carry us very far since we will be unable to decide whether the discrepancies noted are due to the existence of hidden variables or inaccuracies in the data. The crucial problem which confronts us, therefore, has to do with the accuracy of the data.[23] If the latter are reliable, then models can be developed which are capable of describing the interdependence of the variables.[24]

Far from leading us down a false path, as Bull would have us believe, the scientific approach confronts us with the challenge to seek to define and classify our data with diligence and intelligence in order that we can arrive at theories which explain the phenomena we confront.

The scientific approach, however, is not and can never be a substitute for historical explanation. In the first place history provides us with the material with which we form our inductive hypotheses about the data. It is at once the chief stimulus to our construction of theories and the major check upon the wilder and more absurd flights of our theoretical imagination. Respect for the facts is the hallmark of science and in the case of world politics this means historical facts. History therefore resembles a bank. From it we draw our fund of ideas and to history we return to cash our methodological checks, to discover if we have overdrawn our theoreti-cal accounts and to what extent we need to modify or abandon our theoretical drafts. History is the source not only of particular facts which go to make up the structure of our classifications—the mosaic of concepts which structure our understanding—but it alone provides us with the facts which can falsify the propositions we advance as likely candidates for explanation. In these basic activities history is indeed the laboratory in which we work.

In one important manner history stands apart. It serves to remind us that all empirical statements about the world take place in a particular context of time and space, that we always generalize about men and events at our peril. It tells us that there *may* be important differences between events—differences so important and distinct that general statements emerge so qualified as to be relatively unprofitable as guides to explanation. "No study of history can be detailed enough."[25] Why? Because only by studies in depth can we establish the accuracy of the data on which we base our generalizations.

One or two examples will show the force of this contention and its impact on any scientific study of world politics. Suppose we wish to test hypotheses on the role of ideology in alliance formation or whether states seek weaker but more reliable allies as opposed to stronger but less dependable partners? How specifically would we use the British search for an alliance with Poland and then the effort to secure a Russian alliance in the spring of 1939? It was generally agreed that at the end of March 1939 Chamberlain's Cabinet panicked at the news of an impending attack on Poland and, without taking time to weigh the issue carefully, gave Poland a guarantee against German aggression and that the Cabinet, out of a fear of communism and a wish to make a deal with Germany, at no point during 1939 desired a Soviet alliance, merely negotiating with the Russians to deceive public opinion. Detailed research now shows this commonly accepted view to be untrue.[26] The Cabinet, after careful deliberation, chose Poland during the latter half of March despite the contrary advice of the chiefs of staff. By late May, the disastrous consequences of this earlier decision having become apparent, the Cabinet was then converted to accepting the necessity of an alliance with the Soviet Union. Thus, only the correct version of events will enable accurate tests of hypotheses concerning alliance formation, no matter how sophisticated the techniques used,[27] for if the data are false or wrongly classified totally false conclusions will be drawn from the "facts."[28]

The question then arises: "Is our data base accurate enough to test and develop hypotheses?" Only a group of skilled diplomatic historians could answer this question in the richness of detail which it deserves. The general answer is: "Probably not for any but the simplest propositions. As the theory to be tested goes beyond single, clear and limited hypotheses to complex propositions and models which consist of interacting variables, the data will often not enable us to choose among conflicting explanations." This is the chief reason why scholars steeped in the primary sources view much of the effort to test historical generalizations with grave scepticism.

In a similar vein, a recent study[29] has exploded prevailing views about Hitler's decision to invade Greece and Yugoslavia, the reasons usually given for this delay in attacking Russia and the place of reason as opposed to ideology in the emergence of his strategy. Now when generally accepted ideas on two or three particular events in fairly recent history are shown to be mistaken, should we not be sceptical of generalizations which extend over hundreds of events and decades of time? The sensible answer would seem to be "yes."

At the same time the examples cited indicate clearly that the historical and scientific approach complement one another in critical ways. The scientific approach is helpless without accurate data. The historical approach, because of the strong convention that concentrations should be on time-bound particulars, is inhibited in its search for wider generalizations which might throw light on human action. The historian, by ignoring comparative methods and overemphasizing the uniqueness and contingency of his data, can end up with a collection of useless facts. This is not to say that historians always do so, but only that it is a standing temptation produced by intense preoccupation with the particular as opposed to the general. Some outstanding scholars have avoided this evil. Indeed, one of the most brilliant—perhaps *the* most brilliant—series of generalizations about world politics was written by a historian and not a social scientist.[30] In clear, concise language Sorel, a master of the original sources, describes in a few concise pages the workings of power politics and the balance of power, its corroding effects on treaties and all state relations, and ultimately how the destruction of the old Europe occurred.[31] Sophisticated statistical techniques applied to the data might modify a conclusion here and there but it is difficult to believe that the basic picture would be substantially altered.

It is also important for the student to recognize that the scientific approach contains dangers of its own which go beyond the points made so far. It can blind as well as clarify in that the very attempt to render definitions precise—to "operationalize" them—may lead to a selection of facts so distorted as to produce erroneous conclusions. This is the problem opposite that of the ambiguity of concepts which so often vitiates the work of historians.

Suppose, for example, we wish to test hypotheses which explain the outbreak of war as due to changes in the power capabilities of states. We must first ask how we measure state power. Is it by armed forces in being or should we add defense expenditure? population? revenue? trade value? area of the state? If all six factors are used we have to combine these in a single index and this means that we must assign weights to each factor. But is it the case that governments weighed each of these factors in the same manner over long stretches of time? Clearly this simple index then contains clear *possibilities* for error either because we do not have adequate data to decide the question or because there may have been considerable shifts in attitude on the value attached to the various factors. For example, it is difficult to believe that the advance of technology and its growing impact on weapons did not alter attitudes to the importance of population size. Even if these difficulties could be short-circuited, it is likely that a ranking of states based on the above factors with assigned weights might look very different from a ranking which included only armed forces and defense expenditures. An index which includes area and population is clearly a more static index than this last and therefore would not reflect change to anything like the extent of an index which emphasized the build-up of armed forces or defense spending. On the other hand an index based on the last two factors would be highly sensitive to sudden shifts in the military balance, particularly if it were combined with assumptions about the attitude of statesmen to the kind of war likely to ensue. This last point is very important since considerable evidence exists that, at least until quite recent times, political leaders entered war with the expectation of quick and relatively bloodless victories.[32] Hence, the test of any hypotheses which linked changes in power capabilities to the onset of war could have very different results if the definition—and hence the ranking of states—were changed, since the definition is a direct result of the index chosen.[33] Thus, we can see at once that an intimate knowledge of historically-conditioned attitudes would be of immense, indeed indispensable, aid in the construction of accurate indices and models used to test hypotheses. No better example could be found for the assertion that the scientific approach, to be fruitful, requires the active support of scholars steeped in the primary data for the period to be investigated.

Finally, this example should lead us to examine any series of generalizations with care and caution. In particular we must be alert to the question of whether the set of events being compared is *clearly comparable in the sense of operating under similar conditions.* If key conditions begin to change during the period in question, the theory will have to be modified or perhaps discarded. In the latter case we will be forced back upon historical studies of particular events for our understanding.

Our conclusion, therefore, is that the historical approach and the approach of science are not properly viewed as rivals but rather as partners in the search for more accurate understanding. History and science in the study of world politics are united by necessity in a permanent and inextricable alliance.

Conclusion

We cannot see but by being sensible of our blindness.
Edmund Burke
Man is above all else a learning creature and it may
be that we shall find much of the "cause" of a person's
actions in what he has learnt in the past, and the "cure,"
if any is needed, in further learning in the future.
J. Z. Young,
AN INTRODUCTION TO THE STUDY OF MAN (1971)

This book began with an expression of opinion to the effect that whenever men seek to explain any sort of activity or thing whatever, they must, willy-nilly, use a theory. In the intervening pages we have tried to describe and, to some extent, analyze a few of the efforts to render theory explicit. We chose deliberately not to define either the subject or its methods in advance. Rather what we have done is to examine some theoretical efforts by a variety of persons who professed to be interested in what they called "international relations." We have thus, in a sense, let the theories "speak for themselves." In so doing, they have revealed not one approach or one set of problems but quite the reverse. Thus, we have looked at a whole spectrum of theories ranging from those which concentrated on individual, particular elements to theories which tried to present abstract models of entire international systems.

The reader must, of course, decide whether we have done so fairly and effectively. At the very least we would hope that students have come to appreciate the fact that the various theories attempt very different things and help us "understand" the subject in very different ways. There is, in fact, no single "right" way to handle theory. We hope that differing approaches to theory make clear the point that, by and large, theories complement one another in significant ways not only in terms of perspectives but in terms of method. No one approach can possibly exhaust the data nor can such approaches be substitutes for one another. The present state of our knowledge simply does not permit exclusive claim to primacy. The only proper attitude is one of humility before the facts. What is understood (theoretically) is but a small fraction of what is available as raw data. Hence we should welcome all efforts, no matter how diverse, which throw some light on the subject. This is not to say that some explanations have not proven to be better than others, whether "better" be defined in terms of conformity with the known facts or because a particular hypothesis explains more of the facts than another or because a particular approach has produced or shows promise of producing more fruitful ideas than another.

An examination of ethical theory refutes both the simple-minded notion that ethics plays little or no part in international relations or that a few basic principles suffice to guide state policy. Prior ethical choices were found to underly the policies of states and it was demonstrated that morals and interest cannot be separated in the long run. Moral commitments and attitudes do fluctuate over time, depending on knowledge of conditions, the character of statesmen and the scale of sacrifices demanded. The vital importance of ethical issues is best illustrated by the fact that it is ultimately ethical beliefs which are the basic cause of threats to the peace. For it is the desire of men to keep the protection of these basic values in their own hands which leads to their willingness to use force in their defense.

An examination of attempts by jurists, largely through the doctrine of the just war, to mitigate violence, leads to the melancholy conclusion that such attempts have failed. Violence still rages in the relations of states. State imperatives still take precedence over those of an inchoate world community. The basic problem is not one of structure—though structure is indispensable—but of a change in the objectives and attitudes of governing elites and their constituents. This involves a long process of education but an operative code of justice is emerging on a world scale based on the enhancement of the welfare and dignity of the human individual and the development of minimum standards of well-being for the peoples of the world. In this development international law has a critical role to play since ongoing and increasingly complex relations require a body of rules which establishes a framework for behavior. Law provides an indispensable framework not only for the clarification of jurisdictional issues and bilateral relations (the rules of diplomacy) but it also assists in the collective effort to give orderly effect to changing political and technical circumstances, as in questions concerning limits to the continental shelf, the uses of oceanic resources and the military uses of outer space. The law is now struggling, so far without much success, to deal with the dangers implicit in intervention in cases of civil strife. No general willingness exists to accept an overall authority but there is a persistent movement in that direction dictated by the need to find common solutions to problems which defy unilateral efforts.

The behavioral sciences cannot provide a total approach to the theory of international relations. This is so because most of the data on which their approach is based deal with behavior on a different level of analysis. Risk-taking under artificial laboratory conditions is not the same thing as decision-making in a great nuclear crisis. Experts in the international field need to cooperate with specialists in the behavioral sciences in order to produce reliable results. But those who reject behavioral studies outright ought to be candid enough to admit that their own work makes assumptions about the psychology of statesmen, the movements of opinion and the ways in which societies function. It is one thing, therefore, to recognize that more often than not the international environment differs sharply from the conditions studied by the social sciences in domestic situations. It is quite another to rely, as many studies do, on unrefined concepts of common sense as if these could not be improved upon by the study of more refined techniques. While the findings of behavioral studies cannot be applied directly to international relations, they can make us more sophisticated about what we are assuming about human psychology, about the way in which roles affect decisions and, in a host of ways, about the social milieu within which policies are formed and carried out. Some studies—e.g., Burton's on controlled communication—might be viewed as a symptom of our disease and not a cure. In a sense this is true. But from another angle they point out clearly the obstacles which misperceptions throw up in the path of conflict resolution. Once we become aware of this we are made aware of the significance of facts and actions which hitherto we may have ignored entirely or the significance of which we misinterpreted.

Systems theory, however, is another matter altogether. It is, in the main, highly abstract and often uses (in a misleading way) terms from the pure sciences. These theories are often purely formal in the precise sense that they have no content from the real world. Morton Kaplan's theories avoid this latter weakness in part and his balance of power model seems to account for alliance behavior in the nineteenth century with considerable accuracy. It seems to be the case, however, that current attempts to analyze the international system as a whole are premature. Success in this field must wait upon good theories at much lower levels of analysis.

A survey of strategic theory demonstrates that, however elegant or persuasive it might be, if it departs from common sense and what is politically acceptable, it will not be implemented. This was the fate of limited nuclear war theories as well as theories of flexible response which demanded enormous commitments to conventional forces in NATO. It is also clear from the history of the strategic arms race that, while technology *may* provide us with the necessary conditions for stability in deterrence, it cannot provide fully adequate conditions. True stability rests willy-nilly on political decisions which attack the root causes of the arms race. There are, of course, degrees of credibility in deterrence and we forget this at our peril. It is also true that the foundations of nuclear deterrence rest ultimately upon an irrational threat. Men have met this unpleasant fact by avoiding direct confrontation (except in Cuba), by respecting clearly defined spheres of influence, by keeping the nuclear threshold high and, above all, by not engaging in conventional war between nuclear states with its risk of escalation. This basic structure of stability cannot last forever. Meanwhile the great powers must not only learn to limit and control the nuclear arms race but they must build a structure of international security while time remains. This is probably the most difficult and urgent political problem which men have ever faced. There are many possible approaches but it is clear that initial steps will have to leave ultimate control, including the right of withdrawal, to the nation-states involved. But unless knowledge grows along with confidence and consensus, the time available for constructive approaches will ebb away, leaving mankind at the mercy of technological change, accident and miscalculation. Old political habits and our fears carry us along the old pathways of force, strategy and politics. Interest and duty demand the erection of a system of peaceful change.

Finally, we have tried to compare the use of rival sets of explanation. It is our conclusion that historical analysis is still fundamental to our understanding for a variety of reasons. History is the main source of our data and of our hypotheses. It defies easy generalizations and forces us to examine the effects of changing conditions. It warns us against a selection of facts which distorts our problems. It drives us back to primary sources for our answers. It is the indispensable partner of the scientific approach in the never-ending effort of man's search for a more accurate understanding of his world.

This book provides an illustration of the role played by theories in our understanding of the world around us. We are born into a world of nature and of culture which we experience as a world common to all of us. This social world is experienced from the very beginning as meaningful and as one in which we gain our knowledge of other men's actions and motives by analogy with our own. This common-sense knowledge, adequate as a means of coming to an initial understanding of our fellows and of the social institutions which exist, possesses degrees of clarity and insight. In many respects, however, it can be and often is mistaken, as when we discover that the weapons we regard as intended for "defensive" purposes are looked upon by our opponents as "offensive" and intended to do them harm. Only understanding based on a theory of how people behave when they seek security through a threat-system will help us resolve such dilemmas. In short, common-sense knowledge needs to be refined by our experience of the world and by the sophisticated achievements of scientific theory. This is perhaps *the* most important fact about theories and the role they play in understanding. For it is a fact that the world of reality contains beliefs and convictions which are real because they are so defined by the participants. "If men define situations as real, they are real in their consequences."[1] In the seventeenth century, witchcraft was not a delusion but an element in the social reality of men. In a similar fashion, the present international system is at bottom what it is because men choose to define it that way. In the face of drastic threats to survival posed by nuclear weapons and the growing interdependence of nations, they are groping their way to new definitions of reality which, it is to be hoped, will be adequate to the needs of the situation. A vital part in this search will be played by theory.[2]

Notes

CHAPTER 2 : ETHICS AND INTERNATIONAL RELATIONS

1   Percy E. Corbett, *Morals, Law and Power in International Relations* (Los Angeles, California, 1956), p. 2; W. T. Stace, *Man Against Darkness* (Pittsburgh, 1967), p. 160.
2   Grant Hugo, *Britain in Tomorrow's World* (London, 1969), pp. 181–2.
3   Corbett, *op. cit.*, p. 5.
4   Patrick Corbett, "Ethics and Experience," *The Aristotelian Society*, Supplementary volume 43 (1969), p. 10.
5   Quoted in Abraham Kaplan, *American Ethics and Public Policy* (New York, 1963), p. 5.
6   L. Susan Stebbing, *Men and Moral Principles*, L. T. Hobhouse Memorial Lectures No. 13 (London, 1944), p. 14.
7   Kaplan, *op. cit.*, p. 92. Thus what many distinguished critics such as Hans J. Morgenthau are really opposing is "moralism." When applied to the position described here their comments have little validity.
8   *Ibid.*, p. 100.
9   A. C. Ewing, "Ethics and Politics," *Philosophy*, vol. 26 (1951), pp. 19–21. Since both ends and means must be weighed when evaluating an action, some analysts prefer to talk about total consequences.
10 Hans J. Morgenthau, *Politics Among Nations*, 4th edition (New York, 1967), p. 246.
11 Morgenthau, *op. cit.*, p. 246.
12 In order to create the illusion of a nonexistent golden age Morgenthau is reduced to the following argument: that "a common system of arts, and laws, and manners," and a "sense of honour and justice" was a "living reality for Fénelon, Rousseau, and Vattel"! The answer, of course, to this is that none of the gentlemen concerned decided the policies followed by their governments which operated according

to reason of state principles. One could easily collect a similar list of scholars and writers today and make a similar assertion about them which would have equally trivial weight as evidence for an assertion concerning the actions of today's rulers. Perhaps even more astonishing is the statement that the contestants on the international scene in the seventeenth and eighteenth centuries were aware of only "one universal moral code to which they all gave unquestioning allegiance." No evidence is advanced for this piece of dogma nor could there be. See for a more accurate description of the actual state of affairs: Albert Sorel, *L'Europe et la révolution française* (Paris, 1885–1904), vols. 1–3; *The New Cambridge Modern History*, vol. 5 (1961), pp. 10, 117, 123, 466, and vol. 7 (1957), p. 227; J. H. Elliott, *Europe Divided 1559–1598* (New York, 1968), pp. 41, 301; John B. Wolf, *The Emergence of the Great Powers 1685–1715* (New York, 1951), pp. 3, 6, 10, 297. The general picture presented is one in which policy is dominated by reason of state with intrigue, conspiracy, secret agents, cruelty, lying and treachery as the norm.

13   Morgenthau, *op. cit.*, pp. 246, 248.

14   P. E. Corbett, "National Interest, International Organization, and American Foreign Policy," *World Politics*, vol. 5 (October 1952), p. 51.

15   Morgenthau, *op. cit.*, pp. 542–3.

16   Its most characteristic expression can be found in Hegel, *Philosophy of Right*, trans. by T. M. Knox (Oxford, 1945), para. 220–37.

17   Herbert C. Kelman, "The Role of the Individual in International Relations: Some Conceptual and Methodological Considerations," *Journal of International Affairs*, vol. 14, no. 1 (1970), pp. 1–17.

18   See, for example, George F. Kennan, *American Diplomacy, 1900–1950* (Chicago, 1951).

19   The point is clearly made by Stebbing, *op. cit.*, p. 16.

20   Alasdair Morrison, "Justice," *The Aristotelian Society, Supplementary Volume 43* (1969), pp. 116–21. The argument which follows accepts Morrison's point of view in large measure but differs from it in certain respects.

21   Arthur Lee Burns, *Ethics and Deterrence*, Adelphi Paper #69. Institute for Strategic Studies, 1970. In the same series see Paul Friedrich Von Weizsäcker, *The Ethical Problems of Modern Strategy*, Adelphi Paper #55. Institute for Strategic Studies, 1969.

22   Paul Ramsay, *War and the Christian Conscience* (Durham, 1961), and the same author's *The Just War: Force and Political Responsibility* (New York, 1968). See also Robert E. Osgood and Robert W. Tucker, *Force, Order, and Justice* (Baltimore, 1967).

23   Von Weizsäcker, *op. cit.*, p. 4.

24   The basic argument is outlined in R. E. Osgood, *Limited War* (Chicago, 1957).

25   Henry A. Kissinger, *Nuclear Weapons and Foreign Policy* (New York, 1958), pp. 145–68. Dr Kissinger proposed this solution while in academic life. It was embodied in a series of understandings between Nixon and Brezhnev in 1972. During the 1973 war in the Middle East, the Soviet Union, although it knew of the coming conflict well in advance of the event, failed to warn the United States. Dr Kissinger,

then Secretary of State, declared in effect that such a warning was too much to expect!

CHAPTER 3: IDEAS OF JUSTICE IN THE RELATIONS OF STATES

1   This is a concise empirical study of the influence of admittedly ill-defined and culturally differentiated ideas of justice in world politics. We make no attempt here or elsewhere in this book to solve the philosophical, sociological or jurisprudential problems confronting any attempt to formulate a general theory of international justice. A profound analysis of these problems is to be found in John Stone's "Approaches to the Notion of International Justice" in Falk and Black (eds.), *The Future of the International Legal Order*, Vol. 1, pp. 372–460 (Princeton, 1969).

2   A concise account of the development and fortunes of the just war doctrine, with authorities, may be found in P. E. Corbett, *Law and Society in the Relations of States* (New York, 1951).

3   *International Law in an Expanding World*, p. 94.

4   See *U.S. Treaties in Force*, Department of State, 1 January 1975, p. 364.

5   R. P. Anand (ed.), *Asian States and the Development of International Law*, 1972, and R. P. Anand, *New States and International Law*, 1972.

6   John Rawls, *A Theory of Justice*, 1970, is a notable addition to the literature.

7   See for example statements by Mr Pavlov (USSR) and Mr Demchenko (Ukraine) in GAOR, Session III, 1948, Third Committee, pp. 327, 341, 408, 418, 420–1, 430, 447, 449, 672. Thus far the chief result of the human-rights provisions in the Helsinki Declaration of 1975 has been charges of violation. On the Russian side these have taken the form of sharp recriminations of American interference in the internal sovereignty of the U.S.S.R.—another instance of great-power tensions paralyzing efforts to achieve justice in a world community.

8   The precise count was 42 for the Economic and Social Rights and 40 for the Social and Political Rights. See *Multilateral Treaties in Respect of which the Secretary-General Performs Depository Functions*. St/LEG/-SER.D/10,1976.

CHAPTER 4: LAW IN THE RELATIONS OF STATES

1   See for example Richard A. Falk, "The Relevance of Political Context," in Karl W. Deutsch and Stanley Hoffman (eds.), *The Relevance of International Law* (Cambridge, Mass., 1968).

2   The theory and practice to which we refer do not necessarily embody those "general principles of law, recognized by civilized nations" which Article 38 of the statute of ICJ instructs the Court to apply; what we have in mind are doctrines and institutions appearing with minor variations in different, but by no means necessarily all, systems. Of course this clause in the Statute is itself evidence of the reliance

upon municipal analogies that we are attempting to demonstrate.

3 *E.g.*, Hans Kelsen, *Principles of International Law*, 2nd ed. (New York, 1966), pp. 389–95; Sir Hersch Lauterpacht, *Recognition in International Law* (Cambridge, 1943).

4 Cf. Charles De Visscher, *Theory and Reality in Public International Law*, 2nd ed. (Princeton, 1969), pp. 205–6.

5 A definition of aggression was approved by the General Assembly of the United Nations in Resolution 3314 (XXIX), 14 December 1974. No adequate arrangements were made for enforcement. The weaknesses of the Resolution as an instrument of peace are cogently set forth by Julius Stone in "Hopes and Loopholes in the 1974 Definition of Aggression," *A.J.I.L.*, vol. 71, No. 2, pp. 224–46.

6 See above, p. 69.

7 As of 1977 this Conference is still continuing.

8 See *U.S. Treaties in Force*, Department of State, 1 January 1975, p. 412.

CHAPTER 5: THE BEHAVIORAL SCIENCES IN THE STUDY OF CONFLICT

1 R. A. Dahl, "The Behavioral Approach in Political Science: Epitaph for a Monument to a Successful Protest," *American Political Science Review*, vol. 55 (1961), pp. 763–72.

2 K. W. Kim, "The Limits of Behavioral Explanation in Politics," *The Canadian Journal of Economics and Political Science*, vol. 31 (1965), pp. 315–27.

3 Kim, *op. cit.*, p. 316.

4 Susan D. Jones and J. David Singer, *Beyond Conjecture in International Politics* (Itasca, Illinois, 1972).

5 *Ibid.*

6 David Easton, "The Current Meaning of 'Behavioralism'," in James E. Charlesworth (ed.), *Contemporary Political Analysis* (New York, 1967), pp. 11–31. See also Heinz Elau (ed.), *Behavioralism in Political Science* (New York, 1969).

The key methodological points are that (1) units of study (decisions, systems, etc.) do not define a field of study since they are selected by the theory which postulates them and (2) since all theories from the social sciences are partial and incomplete, they are eclectic when approaching empirical problems out of sheer necessity. (See Scott Greer, "Sociology and Political Science," in J. M. Lipsit (ed.), *Politics and the Social Sciences* (New York, 1969), pp. 54–5. Greer argues that there are only two basic analytical schemes for the study of human behavior— the psychological and the sociological—and that their theories are cognate with utility depending on the development of transitivity.

7 This point is made with clarity and force by Herbert Kelman (ed.), *International Behavior, a Social-Psychological Analysis* (New York, 1965), p. 31.

8 Kelman, *op. cit.*, p. 31.

9 *Ibid.*, p. 579.

10 *Ibid.*, p. 580.

11   Kelman, *op. cit.*, chs. 2–8; see particularly pp. 586–94 for a concise summary of the approaches used. For an imaginative and suggestive use of the concept of "images" placed in the full context of international politics, see Robert Jervis, *The Logic of Images in International Relations* (Princeton, 1970).

12   Kelman, *op. cit.*, p. 591.

13   Some of the best experiments have been done by M. Sherif, et al., *Intergroup Conflict and Cooperation* (Norman, Oklahoma, 1961); on simulation experiments see H. Guetzkow, et al., *Simulation in International Relations* (Englewood Cliffs, 1963).

14   Kelman, *op. cit.*, pp. 596–7.

15   Kelman, *op. cit.*, p. 597.

16   *Ibid.*, p. 599.

17   A classic book which contains all these methodological examples is Hans J. Morgenthau, *Politics Among Nations*, 5th ed. (New York, 1973).

18   For a short but brilliant analysis of the logical issues involved, see Nicholas Rescher, *The Primacy of Practice* (Oxford, 1973), especially pp. 3, 14–16, 42–3, 66–7.

19   Rescher, *op. cit.*, pp. 14–15. This view of truth does not require us to deny that human values are involved in either the derivation or application of theories. Clearly the very notions of "control," "survival" and so on are derived from man's view of himself. See Mary Hesse, "In Defence of Objectivity," *Proceedings of the British Academy*, vol. 58 (1972), pp. 275–92. Objective knowledge demands neither the total separation of man from nature nor the converse.

20   See for example H. R. Alker and P. G. Bock, "Propositions About International Relations," *Political Science Annual 1972*, pp. 385–495. Bernard Berelson and Gary A. Steiner, *Human Behavior, an Inventory of Scientific Findings* (New York, 1964), is more easily used since the scientific assumptions on which the propositions rest are clearly indicated. However, very few hypotheses relate directly to international situations.

21   It should be pointed out that the following section does *not* deal with mathematical theories of decision-making. These attempt to arrive at methods of reaching optimum decisions by eliminating subjective elements through the use of formal rules. For a short, incisive treatment of some of the main theories, see D. J. White, *Decision Theory* (Chicago, 1964).

22   Ward Edwards, "Probability-Preferences in Gambling," *American Journal of Psychology* (1953), vol. 66, pp. 349–64 and that same journal, vol. 67 (1954), pp. 441–52; also his "The Prediction of Decisions Among Bets," *Journal of Experimental Psychology*, vol. 51 (1955), pp. 201–14, and "Subjective Probabilities Inferred from Decisions," *Psychological Review* vol. 69 (1962), pp. 109–35.

23   M. G. Preston and P. Baratta, "An Experimental Study of the Auction-Value of an Uncertain Outcome," *American Journal of Psychology*, vol. 61 (1948), pp. 183–93.

24   Dean G. Pruitt, "Pattern and Level of Risk in Gambling Decisions," *Psychological Review*, vol. 69 (1962), pp. 187–201.

25   Edwards, *op. cit.*, (1954), pp. 441ff.

26 Paul Slovic, "Assessment of Risk Taking Behavior," *Psychological Bulletin*, vol. 61 (1964), pp. 220–33.

27 Slovic, *op. cit.*, p. 229.

28 For additional material see John Cohen and Ian Christensen, *Information and Choice* (Edinburgh, 1970); John Cohen, *Psychological Probability* (London, 1972). These studies add a great deal to our understanding of risk but because they show clearly the complexity of risk-taking behavior, they need to be used with great caution. See for example Cohen and Christensen, pp. 74ff. for an evaluation of some experiments. They show that among the variables ignored are: the degree of interest in the gambling situation, belief in luck, the extent to which skill can be used; all of which may significantly affect psychological probability or utility significantly. A model based solely on the latter two factors (probability and utility) could therefore be of little value.

29 J. Cohen and M. Hansel, *Risk and Gambling* (New York, 1956). The authors suggest that the estimate of risk is directly proportionate to the level of fear.

30 Carey B. Joynt, "The Anatomy of Crisis," *The Year Book of World Affairs 1974* (London, 1974), pp. 15–22.

31 Coral Bell, *The Convention of Crisis* (London, 1971), p. 17.

32 For an extended analysis of this general problem, see C. B. Joynt and N. Rescher, "On Explanation in History," 68 *Mind*, pp. 383–8, and by the same authors, "The Problem of Uniqueness in History," *History and Theory*, Vol. 1, pp. 156–7.

33 For a clear exposition of this concept of a hierarchical ranking, see G. Schwarzenberger, *Power Politics* (1951), Chs. 6 and 7. The concept is posited as follows: "In its power aspects, the aristocracy of sovereign states is hierarchic (p. 111)."

34 An excellent example of a fruitful interplay between behavioral studies and case histories is Richard Little, *Intervention. External Involvement in Civil War* (London, 1975).

35 F. M. Thrasher, *The Gang* (Chicago, 1927). See especially pp. 54–6, 173–5, 183–4. Also H. A. Block and A. Niederhoffer, *The Gang* (New York, 1958). There are, of course, great differences between a gang and a state in terms of function.

36 The following will be found extremely useful: Konrad Lorenz, *On Aggression* (London, 1966); Desmond Morris, *The Naked Ape* (London, 1967); N. Tinbergen, "On War and Peace in Animals and Man," *Science*, vol. 160, no. 3835 (28 June 1968), pp. 1411–18; Elton B. McNeil, *The Nature of Human Conflict* (New York, 1965); R. A. Hinde, "The Nature of Aggression," *New Society*, vol. 9 (2 March 1967), pp. 302–4; R. A. Hinde, "Aggression Again," *New Society*, vol. 11 (20 February 1969), pp. 291–2; Jules H. Masserman (ed.), *Violence and War, Science and Psychoanalysis, vol. 6* (New York, 1963).

37 Lee M. F. Ashley Montagu (ed.), *Man and Aggression* (London, 1968).

38 R. A. Hinde (1969), p. 291.

39 N. Tinbergen, *op. cit.*, p. 1414.

40 *Ibid.*, p. 1413.

41 For a short summary see Margaret Mead, "Violence in the Perspective

of Culture History," in Jules H. Masserman (ed.), *Violence and War* (New York, 1963).

42 · For an analysis of the present role of war, see Chapter 8. The major external functions of war have included the protection of state territory, the revision of boundaries, the redistribution of peoples and resources and the final arbiter of power relations.

43 John W. Burton, *Conflict and Communication* (New York, 1969). Also his "The Relevance of Behavioral Theories," in J. N. Moore (ed.), *Law and Civil War in the Modern World* (University of Virginia, 1973).

44 Burton (1969), p. 174.

45 *Ibid.*, pp. 177–8.

46 Burton (1973), p. 13.

47 *Knowledge and Necessity. Royal Institute of Philosophy Lectures* (London, 1970), p. 64.

48 Bert R. Brown, "Reflections on Missing the Broadside of a Barn," *The Journal of Applied Behavioral Science*, vol. 9 (no. 4), 1973, pp. 450–58; B. Brown and J. Rubin, *The Social Psychology of Bargaining and Negotiation* (New York, 1973); Roger Fisher (ed.), *International Conflict and Behavioral Science* (New York, 1964), pp. 91–109.

49 R. S. Baker, *Woodrow Wilson and World Settlement*, vol. 1, p. 112.

CHAPTER 6 : SYSTEMS THEORY : NEW AND OLD

1 Anatol Rapaport, "General Systems Theory," *International Encyclopedia of the Social Sciences*, vol. 15, p. 457. This is the best short treatment of the subject. The pioneer thinker in the field is Ludwig Von Bertalanffy, *General Systems Theory* (New York, 1969).

2 Michael Banks, "Systems Analysis and the Study of Regions," *International Studies Quarterly*, vol. 13 (1969), pp. 347–8.

3 Rapaport, *op. cit.*, p. 456.

4 One of the authors has developed an arms race model which, when reduced to a mathematical equation, is isomorphic with the formula for radioactive decay. This isomorphism is probably a mere coincidence and is likely to remain a theoretical curiosity, nothing more.

5 Jerome Stephens, "An Appraisal of Some System Approaches in the Study of International Systems," *International Studies Quarterly*, vol. 16 (1972), pp. 321–49. Stephens comes close to this demand. Another scholar is quite explicit on the point. See R. C. Buck, "On the Logic of General Behavior Systems Theory," in Herbert Feigl and Michael Scriven (eds.), *Minnesota Studies in the Philosophy of Science*, vol. 1 (Minneapolis, 1956), pp. 223–38.

6 See for example Thomas L. Saaty, *Mathematical Models of Arms Control and Disarmament* (New York, 1968).

7 David Easton, *A Systems Analysis of Political Life* (New York, 1965); *A Framework for Political Analysis* (Englewood Cliffs, 1965) and his *The Political System*.

8 *Framework*, Introduction, p. xiii.

9 *Framework*, p. 74; *Systems Analysis*, p. 24.

10 *The Political System*, p. 132; *Systems Analysis*, p. 212.

11 *Systems Analysis*, Chs. 4 and 10.

12 *Ibid.*, p. 24; pp. 222–4.

13 *Systems Analysis*, p. 222.

14 *Ibid.*, p. 223.

15 *Ibid.*, pp. 223–4.

16 A similar critique could be made of many other key concepts at critical points in the theory but space does not permit any further demonstrations.

17 *Systems Analysis*, p. 487.

18 *Ibid.*, p. 487.

19 *Systems Analysis*, pp. 485–6.

20 *Ibid.*, p. 487. Italics supplied.

21 *Ibid.*, p. 487.

22 For a severe but penetrating analysis, see M. B. Nicholson and P. A. Reynolds, "General Systems, the International System, and the Eastonian Analysis," *Political Studies*, vol. 15 (1967), pp. 12–31.

23 *Ibid.*, p. 23.

24 *Systems Analysis*, p. 349.

25 For a short description of these activities, see George Modelski, *Principles of World Politics* (New York, 1972), pp. 151–61.

26 Modelski (p. 138) estimates that, out of a total of 56 billions devoted by the United States to foreign policy in 1965, 48 went to the military, 4 to intelligence, 3.8 to economic aid, and .2 and .3 to propaganda and diplomacy.

27 Morton A. Kaplan, *System and Process in International Politics* (New York, 1957), and his further explanation and defense in *New Approaches to International Relations* (New York, 1968), pp. 1–18 and pp. 381–404.

28 Charles P. Kindleberger, "Scientific International Politics," *World Politics*, vol. 10 (October 1958), p. 83.

29 Kaplan, "The Systems Approach to International Politics," *New Approaches to International Relations*, p. 388. Hereafter cited as Kaplan (1968).

30 Oran R. Young, *A Systemic Approach to International Politics*, Research Monograph No. 33 (Princeton, 1968), p. 53. Hedley Bull, "International Theory: The Case for a Classical Approach," *World Politics*, vol. 18 (April 1966), argues that not all Kaplan's models are rigorously deduced. Kaplan has explicitly denied any implication of strict deduction (Kaplan, 1957, pp. 245–6). Apart from the obvious fact that an author should not be accused of doing what he has in fact denied, it is impossible to demonstrate precise deduction on a verbal model. Only mathematical models are capable of such demonstration.

31 *Ibid.*, p. 53. Somewhat inconsistently, Young follows this perfectly reasonable demand by the curious assertion that "Kaplan's work veers off toward the discussion of empirical examples . . ." (p. 53, footnote 119).

32 Kaplan (1957), p. 23ff.

33 Kindleberger, *op. cit.*, p. 87.

34 Raymond Aron, *Peace and War* (New York, 1966), p. 129.

35 *Ibid.*, p. 129.

36   Martin Wight, "The Balance of Power and International Order," in Alan James (ed.), *The Bases of International Order. Essays in Honour of C. A. W. Manning* (London, 1973), p. 100.

37   *Ibid.*, p. 104.

38   Kaplan (1968), pp. 396ff. A recent study, however, seems to support Kaplan's theory with respect to alliance behavior. Lee P. J. McGowan and R. M. Rood, "Alliance Behavior on Balance of Power Systems: Applying a Poisson Model to 19th Century Europe," *The American Political Science Review*, vol. 69 (September 1975), pp. 859–70.

39   Kaplan (1957), p. 60.

40   Kaplan (1957), p. 63.

41   Kaplan (1957), p. 89.

42   *Ibid.*, p. 92.

43   Kaplan (1957). Hypotheses (2) and (9).

44   Kaplan (1968), p. 398.

45   Kaplan (1968), p. 398. The reference is to *System and Process*, p. 21.

46   J. David Singer, *A General Systems Taxonomy for Political Science* (New York, 1971) and J. David Singer and Melvin Small, *The Wages of War 1816–1965: A Statistical Handbook* (New York, 1972). These will be referred to as Singer (1971) and Singer (1972).

47   Singer (1971), p. 10.

48   *Ibid.*, p. 20.

49   Singer (1972), p. 16.

50   *Ibid.*, p. 377.

51   Singer (1972), pp. 377–8.

CHAPTER 7: THE INTERNATIONAL IMPACT OF AMERICAN THEORY

1   System = an aggregate of interacting units.

2   For a completely dispassionate comparison of the systems and field theories, see Charles A. McClelland, "Field and Systems Theory in International Relations," in Lepawsky, Buehrig and Lasswell (eds.), *The Search for World Order*, pp. 371–85. On the variety and opposition of various statements of the systems theory, McClelland has this to say: "The idea of system in international relations immediately acquired multiple meanings and references. Contrasting formulations of the systems concept have continued to prevail, although some valiant efforts have been made to summarize, compare, and integrate the elements of theory."

3   Some measure of his success, and of the resulting intellectual disturbance, may be found in the long and troubled review by Henri Meyrowitz, Docteur en Droit and Avocat à la Cour de Paris, in 97 *Journal de Droit International*, Oct.–Dec. 1970, pp. 902–6.

4   See especially pp. 174–95 for Burlatski's discussion of American political scientists.

5   For a striking example of such casuistry among Soviet writers, see the monograph by the young scholar, E. L. Kuzmin, *Mirovoe Gosudarstvo: Illusii ili Realnost?*, I M O, Moscow, 1969.

6　This was written before the publication of Hedrick Smith's superb study, *The Russians*, Ballantine Books (New York, January 1977), which confirms the hypothesis here stated.

7　For an excellent study of the "Concept of the Scientific and Technical Revolution in Soviet Theory" see J. M. Cooper in CREES Discussion Papers, Series RC/C, University of Birmingham Centre for Russian and East European Studies.

CHAPTER 8: FORCE, STRATEGY AND POLITICS

1　World Military Expenditures and Arms Transfers 1966–1975. United States Arms Control and Disarmament Agency (1977), p. 1. This figure is in equivalent constant dollars. The 1966 amount was $285 billion.

2　For a convenient summary, see George Modelski, *Principles of World Politics* (New York, 1972), p. 131.

3　Hence there is no agreed definition of strategy, which ranges from "The art of distributing and applying military means to fulfill the ends of policy" (B. H. Liddell Hart, *Strategy: The Indirect Approach* (London, 1967), p. 335) to those which equate the term with state policy viewed in its entirety. Raymond Aron opts for a modified version of the latter notion: "By strategy I mean the action in cases in which the rules effectively observed do not exclude recourse to armed force." (Raymond Aron, "The Evolution of Modern Strategic Thought," in *Problems of Modern Strategy*, Adelphi Papers No. 54, February 1969, p. 2.) Michael Howard (*ibid.*, p. 8) argues that "it is this element of *force* which distinguishes 'strategy' from the purposeful planning in other branches of human activity to which the term is often loosely applied."

4　Tristam Coffin, *The Armed Society* (Baltimore, 1964), p. 238.

5　Walter Slocombe, "The Political Implications of Strategic Parity," Adelphi Papers No. 77, May 1971, p. 3.

6　P. M. S. Blackett, *Studies of War—Nuclear and Conventional* (New York, 1962), p. 129.

7　Blackett, *op. cit.*, p. 128.

8　This is the conclusion of a Nobel prize scientist with actual experience of operations research. (Blackett, *op. cit.*, p. 130.)

9　To be certain is to exclude some possibilities; to be sure is to exclude some doubts. (See Alan R. White, "Certainty," in *Aristotelian Society*, Suppl. Proc., No. 46, 1972, p. 15.)

10　Michael Howard, "Military Power and International Order," *International Affairs*, Vol. 40 (July 1964); "The Classical Strategists," in Adelphi Papers No. 54 (February 1969); "Changes in the Use of Force, 1919–1969, in Brian Porter (ed.), *International Politics, 1919–1969* (London, 1972), ch. 7; L. W. Martin, "The Changed Role of Military Power," *International Affairs*, Vol. 46 (November 1970), pp. 101–15. The best treatment from a social science perspective is Klaus Knorr, *On the Uses of Military Power in the Nuclear Age* (Princeton, 1966).

11 Martin, *op. cit.*, p. 101.

12 Michael Howard, "Military Power and International Order," *International Affairs*, Vol. 40, no. 3 (July 1964) p. 402.

13 *Ibid.*, p. 403.

14 *Op. cit.*, p. 403. Professor Howard's assertion is based on the existence of what he calls "more limited and effective forms" of military power but this leaves escalation dangers out of account.

15 The case for ABM defenses is, therefore, based on theories of damage limitation.

16 Martin, *op. cit.*, pp. 104–5.

17 Ian Smart, "Alliance, Deterrence and Defence: The Changing Context of Security," *The Year Book of World Affairs, 1972*, pp. 120–1.

18 Bernard Brodie (ed.), *The Absolute Weapon* (New York, 1946), pp. 75–6.

19 Howard, "The Classical Strategists," p. 21.

20 P. Williams, "The Decline of Academic Strategy—A Reappraisal," *Journal of the Royal United Services Institute for Defence Studies*, Vol. 162 (1972), p. 36.

21 Some of the leading works were William W. Kauffmann, "The Requirements of Deterrence," in *Military Policy and National Security* (Princeton, 1956); Bernard Brodie, *Strategy in the Missile Age* (Princeton, 1959); Herman Kahn, *On Thermo-Nuclear War* (Princeton, 1961); and *Thinking About the Unthinkable* (New York, 1962); Thomas C. Schelling, *The Strategy of Conflict* (Cambridge, Mass., 1960) and *Arms and Influence* (New Haven, 1966). Perhaps the most famous of all were Henry A. Kissinger, *Nuclear Weapons and Foreign Policy* (New York, 1957) and Albert Wohlstetter, "The Delicate Balance of Terror," *Foreign Affairs* (January, 1959), pp. 211–34.

22 Benjamin S. Lambeth, "Deterrence in the MIRV Era," *World Politics*, vol. 24 (January 1972), pp. 221–2. Also, Alain C. Enthoven and K. Wayne Smith, *How Much is Enough? Shaping the Defense Program, 1961–1969* (New York, 1971).

23 Albert Wohlstetter, "The Case for Strategic Force Defense," in J. J. Holst and W. Schneider, Jr. (eds.), *Why ABM?* (New York, 1969), p. 122.

24 The case against ABM was made in Abram Chayes and Jerome B. Wiesner (eds.), *ABM—An Evaluation of the Decision to Deploy an Anti-Ballistic Missile System* (New York, 1969).

25 This is admitted by Wohlstetter, *op. cit.*, p. 130.

26 "The US plans to install three MIRV's on each of some 500 Minuteman III ICBM's and ten on each of 496 Poseidon undersea missiles . . . this would boost the total number of strategic warheads to approximately 12,000." Quoted in J. I. Coffey, *Strategic Power and National Security* (Pittsburgh, 1971), pp. 12–13. To give some idea of the enormous destruction available to both sides, it is estimated that 1 percent of the projected Soviet warheads could kill 50 million Americans (Coffey, p. 39). Even an "outmoded" weapon like the B-52 bomber could do enormous damage. If ten of these aircraft delivered their hydrogen weapons, they could kill 20 million Soviet civilians (Coffey, p. 41).

27 Herman Kahn, *On Escalation* (New York, 1965), pp. 57–8. In a previous
book, *Thinking About the Unthinkable* (New York, 1962), Kahn wavers
from asserting the rationality of making threats which it would be
irrational to carry out (p. 45) to clear assertions that it would *not*
be rational so to do (pp. 68, 124, 179, 188–9).

28 Klaus Knorr and Thornton Read (eds.), *Limited Strategic War* (Princeton,
1962). It should be made clear that the authors are not in any
sense advocating such policies but are simply exploring the possibilities
of various alternatives.

29 Paul Ramsey, *The Limits of Nuclear War* (New York, 1963), pp. 17–25.
This is a short but lucidly devastating account of the logical impasse
to which deterrent strategies lead by a prominent ethicist.

30 In Knorr and Read, *op. cit.*, p. 255.

31 The subtlest examination of the possible strategies of commitment
is T. C. Schelling, *Arms and Influence* (New Haven, 1966), ch. 2.
The ablest critique of such strategies is Stephen Maxwell, *Rationality
in Deterrence*, Adelphi Papers No. 50 (August 1968), (London, 1968).

32 See C. B. Joynt, "The Anatomy of Crises," *The Year Book of World
Affairs, 1974*, pp. 15–22.

33 *Dulles to Bohlen*, 29 October 1956. The Soviets were reassured that
the United States had no intention of making a military alliance
with Hungary and the Russian leaders were reminded of the US
offer of a treaty of assurance. The United States government was
told of Russia's determination to crush the rebellion. (*Bohlen to Dulles*,
30 October 1956.)

34 For a sharp attack on the promise of indefinite stability, see Fred
Ikle, "Can Nuclear Deterrence Last Out the Century?," *Foreign Affairs*
(January 1973), pp. 267–85.

35 Apparently these failsafe procedures do not exist on Polaris missiles.

36 Ikle, p. 273.

37 The above statement of the problem is close to the position adopted
in Leonard Beaton, *The Reform of Power. A Proposal for an International
Security System* (New York, 1972), p. 11. It differs only in that he
stresses the dangers of a crisis in which control might be lost, whereas
we include this danger in the wider issues of the limits to deterrent
stability which also encompass risks from technological change, etc.
Later in his book Beaton does give full recognition to the wider
dangers.

38 For example, Grenville Clark and Louis B. Sohn, *World Peace Through
World Law*, 3rd ed. (Howard University Press, 1966). For a later
elaboration of this position, see Richard A. Falk and Saul H. Mendlovitz,
The Strategy of World Order (New York, 1966). The latest demand
for supranational control is Alva Myrdal, *The Game of Disarmament*
(New York, 1976).

39 Beaton, *op. cit.*, especially ch. 1.

40 *Ibid.*, pp. 15–19.

41 *Ibid.*, pp. 156–7.

42 *Ibid.*, pp. 158–9. Beaton's analogy here is the confidence built through
the Nuclear Planning Group of NATO.

43 *Ibid.*, p. 163.
44 *Ibid.*, p. 167.
45 *Ibid.*, p. 226. The use of the word "sovereign" here needs severe qualification. See below.
46 The United States is not only the chief supplier of arms but has never adopted a set of strict standards for nuclear cooperation.
47 The literature on these questions is very large. See for example, "Arms, Defense Policy, and Arms Control," *Daedalus*, vol. 104 (Summer 1975); Anthony Sampson, *The Arms Bazaar* (London, 1977); *The Diffusion of Power*, Adelphi Papers No. 134, particularly the article by Pierre Hassner. The best information and most evenhanded treatment on a yearly basis are the *Strategic Surveys* published by the International Institute for Strategic Studies. The yearly publications of the International Peace Research Institute (Stockholm) also contain useful information. For a clear and sensible analysis of arms control problems in Europe, see J. I. Coffey, *Arms Control and European Security* (London, 1977).

CHAPTER 9: RIVAL EXPLANATIONS IN INTERNATIONAL RELATIONS

1 The above argument is developed in detail in Carey B. Joynt and Nicholas Rescher, "The Problem of Uniqueness in History," *History and Theory*, vol. 1 (1961), pp. 150–62.
2 See J. David Singer and Melvin Small, "Formal Alliances, 1814–1939: A Quantitative Description," *Journal of Peace Research* (1966), vol. 1, pp. 1–32 and by the same authors, "The Composition and Status Ordering of the International System, 1814–1940," *World Politics* (January 1966), vol. 18, pp. 236–82.
3 Edward E. Azar, "Conflict Escalation and Conflict Reduction in an International Crisis: Suez, 1956," *The Journal of Conflict Resolution* (June 1972), vol. 16, pp. 183–201.
4 This point is made with stunning effect by Marion J. Levy, Jr., "'Does It Matter if He's Naked?' Bawled the Child," in Klaus Knorr and James M. Rosenau, *Contending Approaches to International Politics* (Princeton, 1966), pp. 87–109.
5 See for example the brilliant essay by F. H. Hinsley, "The Development of the European States System Since the Eighteenth Century," *Transactions of the Royal Historical Society* (1961) vol. 11, pp. 69–80. This article traces shifts and transitions in the international system and suggests new hypotheses to account for these changes. An equally learned effort is Martin Wight, "The Balance of Power and International Order," in Alan James (ed.), *The Bases of International Order* (London, 1973), pp. 85–115.
6 Nicholas Rescher, *The Coherence Theory of Truth* (Oxford, 1973), pp. 54, 63ff, 230, 243. This book is a detached and profound analysis of the *logic* of the coherence approach to truth. Our application of selected aspects of the argument to historical explanation should not be taken to imply that Professor Rescher's argument is so directed

or that he in any way implies such an application. We believe, however, that it can be so applied and that, taken as a whole, it presents the logical foundations for a better understanding of historical explanation. For a less technical and more general defense of a coherence theory, see A. C. Ewing, *Value and Reality* (London, 1973), pp. 58–64.

7 A convenient source for many of the issues raised here is Patrick Gardiner (ed.), *The Philosophy of History* (New York, 1974). Students who wish to examine more detailed studies should consult the various issues of the journal, *History and Theory*.

8 For such an attempt, see C. B. Joynt, "The Anatomy of Crises," *The Year Book of World Affairs, 1974*, vol. 28, pp. 15–22.

9 Of particular interest to historians would be a psychological analysis of intentions and motives. For suggestions along these lines see Margaret A. Bowden, "The Structure of Intention," *Journal for the Theory of Social Behavior*, vol. 3 (April 1973), pp. 23–46, and by the same author, *Purposive Explanation in Psychology* (Cambridge, Mass., 1972). Also, George A. Miller, Eugene Galanter and Karl H. Pibram, *Plans and the Structure of Behavior* (London, 1970). For a sceptical treatment of intentions, see T. K. Daveney, "Intentional Behavior," *Journal of the Theory of Social Behavior*, vol. 4 (Summer 1974), pp. 111–29.

10 "History and Theory: The Concept of Scientific History," *History and Theory*, vol. 1, pp. 1–31.

11 F. H. Hinsley, *Europe 1870–1914* (forthcoming). Also, Dwight E. Lee, *Europe's Crucial Years* (New England University Press, 1974). For an attempt to use new evidence to shake existing explanations, see Fritz Fischer, *Germany's Aim in the First World War* (London, 1967), and *World Power or Decline* (New York, 1974). In Ch. 1 of the latter book, Fischer summarizes his argument set forth in another massive study, *Krieg der Illusionen* (Düsseldorf, 1969) to the effect that German war-time aims were the logical extension of pre-war goals. A hypothesis of the latter sort is incapable of precise demonstration, hence the continuing debate. What is not in doubt is the major fact that a sharp relative use in German power led Germany into claiming a world·role commensurate with that new power and into a series of miscalculations covering the likely reaction of other great states, particularly Britain. In short, disputes may rage about what other options were available to Germany but we know in fact what options she chose and what the responses of her opponents were to her choices. Room for doubt may remain at the level of emphasis as to the part played by (a) governmental designs, and (b) developments which occurred independently but even here the range of possible disagreement is not as large as appears on the surface.

12 A number of monographs based on extensive use of the primary sources is just now coming into print. See for example an excellent study of British policy toward Japan, Bradford A. Lee, *Britain and the Sino-Japanese War, 1937–1939* (Stanford, 1973). The part played by military leaders is outlined in D. C. Watt, *Too Serious a Business: European Armed Forces and the Approach of the Second World War* (London, 1975). See also a forthcoming study: H. B. Braddick, *The Italo-Ethiopian*

Crisis and the International System, 1934–1936.

13   Major pioneer efforts are Quincy Wright, *A Study of War*, 2 vols.
(Chicago, 1942); on arms races as a cause of war, see L. F. Richardson,
Arms and Insecurity (1960). Wright's studies are being followed up using
sophisticated statistical techniques in the vast "Correlates of War"
project at the University of Michigan. For the first volume in a
series, see J. David Singer and Melvin Small, *The Wages of War,
1816–1865: A Statistical Handbook* (New York, 1972).

14   See for example, F. H. Hinsley, *op. cit.*, Chs. 4 and 8. In the light
of sharp controversy over the origins of the 1914–18 war, this assertion
might be thought to be misguided and naive. There is, however,
a clearly traceable process beginning with outright propaganda, a
revisionist debate and so on which is gradually transformed by more
and more evidence and careful analysis into a coherent account, the
latter being only slightly modified as a few new facts emerge. At
the level of personal ascription of responsibility or on arguments which
attempt to project certain trends and hence account for later policies
and conflicts, doubts still persist. For a summary of the recent debate,
see J. Remak, "1914—The Third Balkan War: Origins Reconsidered,"
Journal of Modern History (September 1971).

15   "International Theory: The Case for a Classical Approach," *World
Politics* (April 1966), pp. 361–77.

16   A long list of examples is cited in W. I. B. Beveridge, *The Art
of Scientific Investigation*, (New York, 1950), pp. 91–108.

17   *Ibid.*, p. 91.

18   See also the interesting account of Eugene P. Wigner, "The Unreason-
able Effectiveness of Mathematics in the Natural Sciences," *Communication
on Pure and Applied Mathematics*, vol. 13 (February 1960), pp. 1–14.

19   For the logical proofs of this assertion see the classic paper, "The
Concept of Truth in Formalized Languages," in Alfred Tarski, *Logic,
Semantics, Metamathematics* (Oxford, 1956), pp. 152–273. I am indebted
to Professor D. J. Hillman, Department of Philosophy, Lehigh University,
for this reference and for his helpful comments on the uses of models.

20   It might be thought that this assertion contradicts the claim (see
above pp. 193, 202) for the coherence account of historical explanation.
It does not do so for several reasons: (1) it is possible to break
down a complex coherence explanation into subsets. For example,
the approach of war in 1914 could be analyzed by a series of models,
one dealing with deductively related hypotheses connecting the changes
in weapons, army mobilization plans and railways to the emphasis
on offensive war, another set relating to alliances, etc.; (2) the adequacy
of the total or entire set would be determined by the adequacy of
the fit between the total set and the event to be explained—in this
case the coming of the 1914 war.

21   Adolph Grünbaum, "Causality and the Science of Human Behavior,"
American Scientist, vol. 40 (1952), pp. 665–75; Carey B. Joynt and
Nicholas Rescher, "The Problem of Uniqueness in History," *History
and Theory*, vol. 1 (1961), pp. 150–62.

22   Bull's additional assertion to the effect that theories and events are

related as cause and effect and thereby contribute to their own falsification and verification is so obscure as to be almost unintelligible. He may be thinking of the role played in social science by the existence of self-fulfilling prophecies which, by becoming known, creates a problem for the reliable testing of social predictions. (See Robert K. Merton, *Social Theory and Social Structure* (Glencoe, 1949), p. 122.) This also occurs in natural science in the shape of servo-mechanisms. The need for an adjusted prediction in such a case is unquestioned. The logical problems involved are dealt with in E. Grunberg and F. Modigliani, "The Predictability of Social Events," *The Journal of Political Economy*, vol. 62 (1954), pp. 465ff. See also the following article: Adolph Grünbaum, "Historical Determinism, Social Activism, and Predictions in the Social Sciences," *The British Journal for the Philosophy of Science*, vol. 7 (1956), pp. 236–40.

23 For a brilliant analysis of the problems of measurement confronting economic theory, see Oskar Morgenstern, *On the Accuracy of Economic Observations*, 2nd edition (Princeton, 1963), pp. 3–130. This book is a mine of shrewd observations on the problem of measurement, and the exposition of scientific theory it contains is both clear and accurate.

24 It is a sobering thought that the history of science is replete with examples of false theories which, at the time of their appearance, seemed to give extremely accurate results. Their ultimate rejection occurred as a rule when they came into conflict with more general theories or when they were seen to be incompatible with one another. (Wigner, *op. cit.*, p. 12.)

25 Martin L. Van Creveld, *Hitler's Strategy, 1940–1941. The Balkan Clue* (Cambridge University Press, 1973), p. 183.

26 Robert Manne, "The British Decision for Alliance with Russia, May 1939," *Journal of Contemporary History*, vol. 9 (July 1974), pp. 3–26.

27 For an able attempt to test propositions about alliances, see Ole R. Holsti (et al.), *Unity and Disintegration in International Alliances: Comparative Studies* (New York, 1973).

28 This general comment is *not* directed at the conclusions or the techniques used in the volume cited above. It does mean, however, that a very detailed examination of the primary data would be needed in order to arrive at an appraisal of the accuracy of the conclusions drawn. Our colleague, R. F. Wylie, has pointed out the importance of securing the original text in any attempt to interpret problems such as the evolution of Chinese communist ideology. Since changes in the texts regularly occur for political purposes, it is imperative to secure original materials if doctrinal change is to be accurately assessed. Otherwise accepted historical "facts" may turn out to be traps for the unwary.

29 Van Creveld, *op. cit.*

30 Albert Sorel, *Europe and the French Revolution*. Translated and edited by Alfred Cobban and S. W. Hunt (London, 1969).

31 *Ibid.*, pp. 35–118. In these few pages Sorel summarizes the methods and results of three centuries of European statecraft.

32 See for example, Geoffrey Blainey, *The Causes of War* (New York, 1973), pp. 47ff and L. L. Farrar, *The Short War Illusion* (Santa Barbara, 1973).

33 Michael D. Wallace, *War and Rank Among Nations* (Lexington, Mass., 1973). Similar problems arise with efforts to test existing balance of power theories using mathematical methods. See Brian Healy and Arthur Stein, "The Balance of Power in International History," *Journal of Conflict Resolution*, vol. 17 (March 1973), pp. 33–61.

CONCLUSION

1 W. I. Thomas, *The Child in America* (New York, 1927), p. 572.
2 An important new area of theory not discussed in this volume is the subject of international economic relations in its impact on political life. See Roger Morgan (ed.), *The Study of International Affairs* (London, 1972), particularly the stimulating chapter by Susan Strange. Also J. E. Spero, *The Politics of International Economic Relations* (New York, 1977) and D. H. Blake and R. S. Walters, *The Politics of Global Economic Relations* (Englewood Cliffs, N.J., 1976). A highly specialized study is Andrew Shonfield and Hermia Oliver, *International Economic Relations of the Western World, 1959–1971*, 2 vols. (London, 1976).

Subject Index

air,
    International Commission for Air
        Navigation, 43
    International Civil Aviation
        Organization, ICAO, 43
    Paris Convention on Air Naviga-
        tion, 1919, 43
    Chicago Convention on Civil Avi-
        ation, 1944, 43
    sovereignty over air space, 43
    ICAO and the two-freedoms
        agreement, 43
    ICAO and hijacking, 43–4
    punishment of hijacker, Hague
        Conference, 1970, 44

balance of power, 71, 78
    Kaplan and, 71–4
    Wight and, 72
behavioral sciences, 49–64
    and aggression, 60–1
    and analysis of risk-taking, 52–4
    conflict resolution, 61–4
    contributions of, 50
    controlled communication, 61–4
    decision-making and, 52–4
    definitions of, 49–50
    experimental findings and actual
        crises, 54–9
    limitations of, 50, 52, 54

    suggestions for new research, 59,
        60
    uses of experiments, 51–4

canon law, on just and unjust war,
    20
Concert of Europe, an experiment
    in supranational constitution,
    32

Decretium Gratiani, on just and un-
    just war, 20
deterrence, 89–95
    credibility and, 95
    great powers and, 97
    stability of, 91–2
    technology and, 92–3, 96
diplomacy, 40
    Vienna Conventions of 1961 and
        1963 on diplomatic and con-
        sular interchange, 41

environmental pollution, 48, 79
    Conference on the Human En-
        vironment, Stockholm, 1972,
        48
ethics, 4–19
    as a threat to peace, 19
    ends and means, 7
    ethical principles, nature of, 6

Name Index